BEHOLD

ALL THINGS AM BECOME

NEW

(II CORINTHIANS 5:17 KJV)

GEORGE J. CUNNINGHAM, SR.

AmErica House
Baltimore

First printing

ISBN: 1-58851-214-2
PUBLISHED BY AMERICA HOUSE BOOK PUBLISHERS
www.publishamerica.com
Baltimore

Printed in the United States of America

This book is dedicated to my favorite daughter, Monette, who has unselfishly given me good and abundant help in finalizing the book; to her three brothers, Charles, George Jr., and Tommy; and especially to my good Christian wife Pluma, who has given me such precious presents from God as our four Christian children.

The ACKNOWLEDGEMENT

A prayer on every page. During the preparation of this manuscript, I prayed daily for God's help because I saw a real need to prepare a training course which could help prevent the loss of new converts. It seemed that many of them, essentially neglected, slipped quietly out of Christianity and back into the world from which they had most recently emerged. What could be done to save them? Looking over related material, I saw that some books amounted to no more than extended pep talks with very little substance. Other books seemed to present a challenge but were too narrow in scope. Thus after much prayer, I decided to prepare a course which I hoped would be more suited to the needs of new converts, yet challenging enough to train others at various stages of development.

In the preparation of this course, I borrowed generously from many lessons that I had composed in the last 40 plus years of teaching Bible classes. In preparing and teaching each of these lessons I had prayed for, and received help from our Lord Jesus Christ. For His help on these lessons and His help in the writing of this manuscript, I thank you, Lord.

And lest the Lord be criticized for His help, let me say that anything praiseworthy is a gift from the Lord; and anything that is not suitable is the result of me not having the wisdom nor the courage to turn it all over to the Lord.

I would also like to thank the following people for their good and appreciated help:

❖ My dear wife, Pluma, who showed unending patience and understanding as I frequently neglected her during the preparation of the manuscript.

❖ My typists: Mrs. Monette Rice, Mrs. J.J. Anderson, Mrs. Jan Crowley, Mrs. Shiryl Hicks, and my dear wife, who succeeded in spite of my amazingly poor handwriting. Thanks Ladies! You did a good job!

❖ Our preacher, Mr. Michael Harbour, whose sermons inspired me to work harder for the Lord until my "early retirement" <u>which will come only in heaven.</u>

❖ The ladies of the Church whose classes I have taught for several years and who have opened my eyes to the fact that our ladies are the hardest-working non-professional members of the church.

❖ And most of all to the Lord Jesus, my lawyer (I John 2:1), who daily pleads my case in heaven and whose blood is applied daily to sanitize me from my sins.

Thank you, Lord!

FOREWORD

During World War II, after Sir Winston Churchill had given one of his now celebrated speeches, he was severely criticized by a host of grammarians. Sir Winston, never lacking in wit, quickly retorted: "This is criticism up with which I will not put." In effect, he was ridiculing the grammarians.

I personally would not ridicule formal grammar. There is a real need for it in courses of English, History, Law, Science and many other courses at college level. I myself have a teaching minor in English and I do value formal grammar in its place.

But I clearly remember an event that took place in Jr. College in 1941. A young lady was assigned to teach both English and Speech. While directing a play, she used a great deal of slang and otherwise clearly butchered the Queen's English. When a student in the class called attention to the teacher's grammatical misdemeanors, the teacher had this defense: "Yes, I teach English, but I also teach speech and what I said clearly communicated." And she was right!

Yes, I appreciate formal grammar, but the Air Force converted me. While writing extension courses and other training courses, I learned that grammatical correctness was not "the sacred cow" but that clear communication was indeed the purpose of all writing. I also learned to keep a conversational tone in my writing to avoid a stilted, pedantic and numbing effect on the readers.

Thus, in my writing you will find such horrible grammatical sins as the following:

❖ Split infinitives.
❖ Sentences ending with prepositions.
❖ Sentence fragments.
❖ Sentences beginning with "and" and "but".

- ❖ The use of such "dead" words as "Well" and "say."
- ❖ But hopefully NO MISPLACED MODIFIER.

If I have offended any grammarian, please accept my apology; and if I have pleased any communicator, please accept my thanks for your praise.

CONTENTS

Chapter I. <u>ON YOUR MARK, GET SET, GROW,</u>

Section 1: <u>Let's Talk About It.</u>

"Desire the sincere milk of the word that you may grow." (I Peter 2:2)

Now that you have become a new child of God, welcome to the world of Christianity. It is a bright, new world for you because your past sins have all been forgiven. Yes, it's a bright new world, but because of its very newness, it may seem a little strange and scary at first. But don't be alarmed! All kinds of help are available to ease you over the rough spots and around the potholes that may line your path. And there WILL be some rough spots. Since you are now clean, you want to escape splashes from those potholes, too, don't you? And you strongly desire to grow to be a strong Christian. That desire is not only very commendable but also extremely vital, because a Christian must either grow or perish.

EITHER GROW OR PERISH

"Give diligence to make your calling and election sure." (II Peter 1:10)
"Grow in the grace and knowledge of the Lord Jesus Christ" (II Peter 3:18)
Why did the apostle Peter address these commands to <u>fellow Christians</u> who had already obtained a faith like his own? (II Peter 1:1) He wanted to encourage them to grow, since it was a case of either grow or perish. Even the Lord Jesus himself grew. As he went through his teenage years, "Jesus increased in wisdom and stature and in favor with God and man" (Luke 2:52). Likewise, each of us Christians must continue to grow. Otherwise we will "forget that we have been purged from our old sins" and

11

will "fall away from Christ" (II Peter 1:9, 10). So you see it's either grow or perish; and to complicate things, there are dangers, hindrances, and barriers to our faithfulness and to our growth. For example, if you are like most of us when we first became Christians, you probably brought with you some old habits and attitudes which could weaken your efforts to grow.

HABITS AND ATTITUDES

How do you know whether a specific habit or attitude is harmful or beneficial? Go to the answer book – The Bible. At various places in the Bible you will find commands and examples which help us to classify habits and attitudes as either harmful or helpful. We could not cover all of these commands and examples here, of course, but let's call your attention first to some helpful habits and attitudes and then to some harmful ones.

Helpful Habits and Attitudes

Two very helpful habits for a Christian are the habits of regular church attendance and the habit of daily Bible study. With such habits, a Christian can gain God's rating of "NOBLE" (Acts 17:11). Remember, that every chance you have to study the Bible, whether in class or in private, is a chance to grow. Take advantage of each chance by approaching Bible study with the right attitude.

What is the right attitude? It is an attitude which is reverent, prayerful, open-minded, and obedient. Our attitude should be reverent because all Bible study is based on communication from God (II Timothy 3:16-17); and when an all-powerful, all-wise, and loving God speaks, shouldn't we listen carefully and reverently? Our attitude should also be prayerful: We should ask God to help us understand those Bible truths which are most needful for us at our present stage of growth. Our attitude should also be

12

open-minded. We should not cloud the meaning of God's Word by looking at it through any of our own preconceived ideas, but should have the attitude of Eli who said, "Speak Lord, thy servant heareth" (I Samuel 3:9). And finally, we should approach a study of God's Word with an obedient attitude: "Command Lord, and I will obey." If we study God's Word without the intention of obeying it, we will soon forget what we have read; we will be deceiving our own selves; and we will not obtain the blessing of growth (James 1:22-25).

Now that you know the right attitude for <u>Bible</u> study, let's look closely at some additional habits and attitudes which will be helpful in your Christian growth. The following lists of some habits and attitudes that Christians should strive to develop. This is not a complete list but the ones given should provide a good starting place for your growth as a Christian. This list, derived from Colossians, chapter 3, verses 10-15 is presented here, along with other scripture references:

- ❖ <u>Impartiality.</u>   Don't discriminate against a fellow Christian because of race, financial status, or previous background (Galatians 3:28).
- ❖ <u>Compassion.</u> Don't be envious. Rejoice with those who rejoice. Weep with those who mourn (Romans 12:15).
- ❖ <u>Kindness.</u>   Be thoughtful and tender in your association with other people (Ephesians 4:32).
- ❖ <u>Humility.</u> Think of other people as being better than yourself (Philippians 2:3)
- ❖ <u>Gentleness.</u>   Avoid harsh words and action (I Thessalonians 2:7).   Make certain that your words are soft and sweet. (They taste better if you have to eat them.)

❖ <u>Patience.</u> After you fail, keep on trying. Don't condemn yourself. You probably will succeed the next time (Luke 21:19).

❖ <u>Bearing with one another.</u> (I Corinthians 13:7) Don't gossip. Keep quiet about other people's sins and shortcomings.

❖ <u>Forgiveness.</u> Don't hold grudges. Otherwise, Christ will not forgive your sins (Matthew 6:14, 15). Tactfully communicate <u>in private</u> with the person you believe has sinned against you (Matthew 18:15-17). Don't gossip no matter how hurt your feelings are.

❖ <u>Love.</u> Seek the highest good for each person, whether Christian or non-Christian. Try to stimulate each person to Christian love and good works (Hebrew 10:24).

❖ <u>Peace.</u> Let the peace of God rule in your heart. Be content with what you have (I Timothy 6:6). Live a Godly life to escape the torment of an aching conscience.

❖ <u>Gratitude.</u> Be grateful for what the Lord has done for you. He saved you, a helpless sinner, by dying in your place. We should be grateful. Giving the Lord His well-deserved gratitude will help to strengthen both your love for Him and your faith in Him.

Say, that's a pretty big order. That's a lot of good habits and attitudes to develop. But there are also a lot of bad habits and bad attitudes that a Christian should strive to overcome because they darken his life and limit his Christian growth.

Harmful Habits and Attitudes

Since there is a chance that some of us may have some harmful habits and attitudes, let's talk about overcoming them. Please don't be offended by this discussion. Even Christians older than you in the faith must fight bad habits and attitudes. Remember that a church is NOT a gathering place for perfect people (I John 1:8). Instead, a church is a hospital for Christians with various degrees and various kinds of spiritual illnesses-illnesses we are constantly striving to cure. Please join us in our fight against Satan.

Now that we have made this explanation, let's look at a list of harmful habits and attitudes derived from Colossians, chapter 3, verses 5-9. This is by no means a complete list, but the items listed below should be enough to start you on a program of growth to overcome any of these harmful habits and attitudes that you might have.

❖ <u>Immorality.</u> Any sexual activity outside of marriage.

❖ <u>Impurity.</u> Using vulgarity. Taking the Lord's name in vain. Telling or listening to dirty (off color) jokes.

❖ <u>Passion.</u> A sin of the heart. Lusting after sexual contact (Matthew 5:27,28)

❖ <u>Evil Desire.</u> Strongly desiring anything that is harmful in living a Christian life. (Another sin of the heart.)

❖ <u>Greed.</u> A sin of the heart. Desiring material gain (money or possessions) strongly enough to grumble about the lack of it or strongly enough to want to disobey God to obtain it.

❖ <u>Anger.</u> Anger has a natural cycle: first a flash then a gradual subsiding. But if pride feeds it beyond the natural cycle, we have sinned. (Jesus himself was angered but did not sin (Mark 3:5). So we, too, can be angry without sinning (Ephesians 4:26), provided that the anger does not lead us to do wrong and provided that pride does not extend beyond its natural cycle.

❖ <u>Wrath.</u> Anger bursting into action. Don't do it! Exercise self-control.

❖ <u>Malice.</u> Holding a grudge, hidden or unhidden, with the hope of someday getting even. The bedrock of malice is lack of forgiveness, which can condemn our souls (Matthew 6:14-15).

❖ <u>Slander.</u> Speaking evil falsely of a person who usually is absent. (Whether true or false, evil should never be spoken of anyone.)

❖ <u>Abusive speech.</u> Harshly critical language should never be used by a Christian. A Christian should always speak the truth <u>in a loving way</u> (Ephesians 4:15).

❖ <u>Lying.</u> Telling something that is false, <u>including flattery of a person</u> (Psalm 12:2, 3). An <u>honest</u> complement however is highly desirable.

Were you burdened by any of these sinful habits and attitudes before you became a Christian? If so watch out for their reappearance and be prepared to fight them until you overcome.

<u>OVERCOMING HARMFUL HABITS & ATTITUDES</u>

Since you are a Christian, the overcoming of harmful habits and attitudes will be easier for you now, because you have the help of the Lord Jesus Christ. But you still must do your part in fighting to overcome sinful habits and attitudes. Here are four suggestions that might help you.

George J. Cunningham, Sr.

First, Confess Your Faults One to Another
(James 5:16) this is very contrary to worldly "wisdom"
which says to hide your weaknesses. But God knows best.
Why? For one thing, when you confess a fault, you are less
likely to repeat that fault again. But even if you do repeat
the fault and keep confessing it the confessions seem to
give a person more strength for the battle against the fault.
But the main reason for confessing a fault is that the Lord
said to do it. He is always right! So do it!

Second, pray one for another.
When you ask for the prayers of your brothers-in-
Christ, you are tapping into a great deal of prayer power.
And don't forget to pray for yourself, too. With all those
prayers you are mightily strengthened to overcome any
stubborn harmful habit or attitude. Prayer does change
things!

Third, study God's word.
Strength and comfort flow into our souls as we hear
the Good Lord speak to us in the Bible (II Timothy 3:16-
17). After all, Jesus defeated the Devil by quoting
scripture; so scripture must be powerful in its effect. Let us
again point out the importance of church attendance and
daily Bible study, which can arm you with scriptures, a
powerful weapon for your battle against Satan.

**And fourth, don't let your love for Christ grow
cold.**
What could cause our love and faith to lose its
ardor? At least three things.
First, by failing to obey what we learn in Bible
study, we may fool ourselves but we cannot fool God.
Because of our failure to obey, He will not bless us with
growth in love and faith.

Second, if we fail to do good work for which we are created in Christ Jesus (Ephesians 2:10), our faith will soon die (James 2:17). A dead faith, like anything else dead, cannot grow but will also cause our love to die.

Third, because evil abounds in the world, the love of many will grow cold. To prevent evil from chilling our love for Jesus, the Bible gives these commands in Psalm 37:1-8:

- ❖ Don't be envious of wrong doers; otherwise you may soon join in their evil deeds.
- ❖ Don't fear wrong doers. On His own timetable God will punish them.
- ❖ Don't fret because of sinners; such fretting can lead to sin. Instead of fretting, resort to prayer (Philippians 4:6) and think about more pleasant things (Philippians 4:8).

ADDITIONAL HELP IN GROWING

To give you more help in growing this book offers twelve additional chapters related to your relationship with God, God's Blessings, God's Word, Church leadership, your spiritual family, your physical family, the world and worldliness, worldly authorities, prayer, the Lord's Supper, cross carrying and growth in the Christian Graces. Each of these chapters cover a vital area of your Christian relationships and each should be helpful to you in your desire for Christian growth.

Say, we have really covered a great deal of ground in our discussion of Christian growth. And to help you remember more of it, we have a review section titled, "Let's see what you have learned." Be sure to answer all the questions.

But, before you start, let's make some suggestions that will help to make this review section as well as other sections of this book easier for you.

First, to more easily locate any book in your Bible, we suggest that you do the following:

1. Carefully remove pages 309 & 310 from the back of this book.
2. Then, using a pencil, write down, in the appropriate part of the chart, the page number of the first page of each Book of <u>your</u> Bible.
3. Insert your completed chart in a plastic page protector to preserve the chart life and neatness.
4. The plastic page protector can serve as a marker for your book, and since the books are listed in alphabetical order, you can more quickly locate the page number of the desired book in your Bible. Complete your chart now! We'll wait for you!

By the way, some teachers recommend that you memorize the names and order of all the books of the <u>Bible</u>. And such memory work is indeed helpful. But I believe that normal usage will soon acquaint you with the location of most Bible books. Furthermore, memorizing useful Bible verses will, in my opinion, be more helpful for you. After all, when Jesus was tempted by Satan (Matthew 4:1-10), he did not say, "Genesis, Exodus, Leviticus, Numbers…" Instead, He quoted verses that applied to the situation – verses He had memorized. And if you wanted to show a friend how to be saved, would you say, "Matthew, Mark, Luke, John….", or would you tell him the location of the <u>Bible</u> verses which explain how to be saved?

Obviously, a knowledge of Bible verses is more useful, isn't it?

Now, before you go to the review section, let's point out the third section of each chapter. This section, titled: "Section III, Now, Let's Get Personal," will help you to complete a personal inventory and set up goals for Christian growth. It's important that you complete Section

III to the best of your ability. It will help to direct your growth into very useful channels.

Also, notice near the end of Section III that there are <u>Bible</u> verses, selected for their usefulness at this particular stage of your growth. You should memorize not only each verse but also <u>where that verse is located in the Bible.</u> Such memory work will not only make you stronger as a Christian but will also prepare you for Christian influence on both Christians and non-Christians.

<u>Section II: Let's See What You've Learned</u>

1. Two reasons that a Christian must grow are:

    a. God has told us to

    _____ (II Peter 3:18).

    b. If we do not grow, we will be

    _____ and _____ and will

    _____ (II Peter 1: 8-10).

2. How do you know that there are no perfect people living on earth today?

    _____ (I John 1:8; Romans 3:23).

3. Since no one is perfect, is this a suitable excuse for failing to overcome sin in our life? What does God say about it? Be _____ as I am _____ (Matthew 5:48) and be _____ as God is _____ (I Peter 1:14-16).

4. Some helpful habits and attitudes that a Christian should try to develop are _____, _____, _____, _____._____, _____, _____, _____, _____._____, _____ (Colossians 3: 10-15).

5. If a brother-in-Christ has sinned against you, how should you attempt to correct him?   First, _____;   then   _____;   and   finally _____ (Matthew 18:15-17).

6. Christian love seeks the highest good for each person by attempting to stimulate each person to _____   and   _____   _____ (Hebrew 10:24).

7. Some of the harmful habits and attitudes that a Christian   should   strive   to   overcome   are _____, _____, _____._____, _____, _____, _____, _____._____, _____ (Colossians 3: 5-9).

8. Some   of   the   types   of   impure   speech   are _____,   _____,   _____,   or _____   to   _____,   and   taking _____.

9. The rule of thumb that most nearly describes what Christian Speech should be is to

    _____ (Ephesians 4:15).

10. Three rules for overcoming harmful habits and attitudes are

    a. Confess _____, (James 5:16),

    b. Pray _____, (James 5:16), and

    c. Study _____, (II Timothy 3: 16-17).

11. To keep ones love for Christ from growing cold a person should:

    a. _____, (James 1:25),

    b. _____, (James 2:17), and

    c. _____, (Philippians 4: 8).

12. Verses to Memorize:

    a. II Peter 3:18

    b. Acts 17:11

    c. Matthew 6:14, 15

    d. Ephesians 4:15

Section III: Now, Let's Get Personal

1. In your opinion, why is it worthwhile to memorize Bible verses which tell a person how to become a

Christian? _____

(Matthew 28: 19-20).

2. List here those harmful habits and attitudes, if any, which you have carried over from your pre-Christian days. _____

Tell how you plan to overcome them.

_____

3. What, if anything, do you do or say which might cause a fellow Christian to stumble spiritually?

_____

How do you plan to remove from your words and actions these causes of stumbling?

_____

(Pray that God will reveal to you any cause of stumbling for which you are guilty and that He will help you to overcome this weakness.)

4. What is your most besetting sin – the one you are most apt to commit? _____

How do you plan to overcome it?

_____

5. What is your opinion of an older Christian who you see sinning? _____ How should you feel and react to his sin?

_____

6. Do you fret because you see so much evil in the world? _____ What could be the result of such fretting? _____ How do you prevent yourself from fretting? _____

   What should be your attitude toward the evil you see? _____

7. To grow in the grace of the Lord Jesus Christ means that we improve our ability to treat other people and God the way that Jesus would treat them. What will you do while attempting to make such improvements?

   _____

   _____

   _____

   _____

8. Did you become a Christian to escape hell or to show your love for the Lord? _____ As you grow in faith, do you think that your answer to this question will change?_____ Please explain: _____

   _____

   _____

   _____

9. Verses to Memorize:

    a. Romans 3:23

    b. Romans 6:23

    c. Hebrews 11:6

    d. Romans 10:17

    e. Hebrews 5: 8,9

    f. John 3:16

10. After studying 9c – 9f (above) how would you define a saving faith?

_____

_____

_____

_____

Chapter II. <u>YOUR NEW RELATIONSHIP WITH GOD</u>

<u>Section 1: Let's Talk About It.</u>

"Trust in the Lord with all thine heart; and lean not unto thine own understanding." (Proverbs 3:5)

To feed a rooster would you give him hay and wonder why he would not eat? Or would you try to get a horse to occupy the roost in a hen house? The answer to each of these questions is, of course, a resounding NO! To be successful, our actions and expectations must be tailored to fit the nature of the animal of which we speak. Because of their nature, we know a rooster does not eat hay and that a horse cannot occupy a roost in the hen house, whether or not he devoutly desires to do so.

Now the Lord is neither a rooster nor a horse, but the same statement applies equally to a Christian's relationship with God: Before we can see what our relationship is we must first know the nature of God – what He is like --; we must also know our own nature as a human being. Then, knowing these two things --God's nature and our own nature – we can more easily see what kind of relationship should develop between God and us.

In this chapter we discuss three things: (1) the nature of God, (2) the nature of human beings, and (3) the relationship that should exist between God and man.

THE NATURE OF GOD

With the exception of Jesus and the Holy Spirit, no one can completely understand the nature of God because God's ways and thoughts are not the same as our ways and thoughts: They are on a much higher plain than ours (Isaiah 55: 8-9). But God in His wisdom has revealed enough of His nature so that we humans may know how to walk in a good relationship with Him. What has God revealed to us concerning His nature? What does the Bible record about God? The Bible tells us that God is eternal, all-powerful, all knowing, unchanging, good, providential, dependable, loving, jealous, truthful, and just. Let's briefly discuss each of these characteristics of God's nature.

God Is Eternal

With so much rot, decay and death in this world, it is hard to visualize anything that is eternal. But God is! He existed before the creation of the world (Genesis 1:1), and He will still exist long after the world has been destroyed (Revelations 22:1,6). Or as the Psalmist David wrote: "From everlasting to everlasting thou art God" (Psalms 90: 1,2 and Psalms 93:2). God will never die nor leave us.

God Is All-Powerful

He is capable of any creation or of any destruction He chooses to make. He created the heavens and earth by merely speaking them into existence (Genesis 1: 3,6,9,11,14,20 and 24: the "let there be" verses). And He destroyed people and cities as He deemed necessary. For example, since the world at one time was hopelessly locked in evil, He destroyed all but eight people in the "Great Flood" (Genesis 6 and 7). Also He destroyed Pharaoh's army when they attempted to pursue the children of Israel on dry land through the Red Sea (Exodus 14). And He destroyed the sinful cities of Sodom and Gomorrah with fire and brimstone (Genesis 19:24,25). Whatever is necessary, God has the power to accomplish it, whether creation or destruction. We can depend on His strength and knowledge.

God Is All-Knowing

God is all knowing because He exists everywhere and because of His superior knowledge and wisdom. God exist everywhere, in all parts of the earth – on the highest mountain and in the deepest sea. And God can see under all conditions – day, night, fog or clear (Psalms 139:7-12). How then can a person flee from the presence of God or hide from Him? He cannot, as Jonah discovered when he tried to avoid an assignment given to him by God. (Book of Jonah). But Jonah became the main entree in the belly of the big Fish, and decided maybe he had better take God's assignment after all. (Good choice, Jonah!) He finally yielded to God's superior power, knowledge and wisdom.

Why is God so wise? Why does He know us so well? One reason is because He knew us even before our birth. And even then, He knew exactly how long we would live and how our life would turn out (Psalms 139:1-16 and Isaiah 46:10). He knows our every thought and our every word before it is spoken. And if our words and thoughts displease God, He is good enough to tell us, and thus keeps us from floundering deeper and deeper into sin.

God Is Good
Matthew 19:17 records Jesus as saying "there is none good but one, that is, God." And in Romans 3:12 we read that "there is none that doeth good, no, not one." For what reason can we say God is good and man is not? The answer is God is providential, unchanging, dependable, loving, truthful, and just; but man does not always possess these qualities. Let's briefly discuss each of these qualities of our good Heavenly Father.

God Is Providential
In chapter 3, we discuss God's providence, His blessings, in more detail. Here let us quickly point out that God provides for all our needs (not our wants, but our needs). Not only does God provide for our material needs of food, clothing and shelter; but He also provides us with a marvelously made body that is capable of using and enjoying these material blessings. Then, too, He provides

for our spiritual needs: the example Jesus lived, his death, the administration of chastisement when we need to change our ways, and the Holy Spirit to guide us by means of the pages of God's unchanging word, the Bible.

God Is Unchanging

God has no need to change because He is without fault. Also, He has devised a number of rules in the Bible that provide perfect guidance in this sinful world and a perfect basis for judgment in the world to come. God does not change; and like Jesus, He is the same yesterday, today,, and forever (James 1:17, Hebrew 13:8). How thankful, too, we should be that God does not "change the rules in the middle of the game." We can depend upon his fairness.

God Is Dependable

God does what He says He will do - whether it is a blessing or a punishment. Therefore, it is better to trust God than to put your confidence in man (Psalms 118:8). Not only will God "keep the same rules throughout the game," but if he says He is on our side, He will be there to help us when help is needed. He can be depended upon. God's loving care will never desert us.

God Is a Loving God

In, fact, the apostle John declares that "God is love" (I John 4:8). And God shows His love for us in many ways, granting to us both physical and spiritual blessings. But like a good Father, God exhibits "tough love" towards us as He punishes us for our misdeeds (Hebrew 12:5,6) and denies to us those harmful things which we want and sometimes pray for. God's Agape type love is designed to promote our higher good – to help us grow toward Christian maturity by provoking us to love and good works (Hebrew 10:24). And the crowning evidence of God's love for us was the sacrifices of Jesus on the cross for our benefit (John 3:16). Yes, God's love for us brings us many generous gifts – gifts for which God wants to receive credit. And if another claims credit for the gifts from God, God does not appreciate such stealing of credit.

God Is a Jealous God

That God is a jealous God is stated in the very first of the Ten Commandments (Exodus 20:4,5). Since God made us, He alone is entitled to our worship. Today, very few people actually bow down to graven images in this country; but a thing does not have to be a graven image to become an idol. For example, covetousness (greed) is called idolatry in Colossians 3:5. In fact, anything we love more than God and depend upon more than God has become an idol for us. How do we know we love something more than God? If we love God more than the thing, we will obey God (John 14:15) rather than disobey God in order to "enjoy" the forbidden thing. And a jealous God will not let such idolatry go unpunished. God wants us to worship Him and for that worship to be in spirit and in truth.

God Is Truthful

God always tells the truth. He cannot lie. In fact, God's Word, the Bible is called Truth (John 17:17). Not only does God speak the truth, but He also speaks the whole truth. For example, He commands us to support the work of the Church liberally (II Corinthians 9:6), which means that, if possible, we should give 10% or more of our income to the Church. (Jewish people gave about 30%.) However, we are commanded two additional things:

❖ Pay your debts (Roman 13:8)
❖ Care for your family's needs (I Timothy 5:8)
   (Notice this is NEEDS not LUXURIES.)

So you see, God has set up boundaries on the left and boundaries on the right to keep us on the straight and narrow: (Just like the two fences of a cattle chute used to direct cattle into the "BIG PEN."). God has told us the whole truth: we should give generously to the Lord without cheating on our debts or denying our family the NECESSITIES of life. You can see then that God keeps us informed on what we should give. The same is true of other things - God keeps us informed. He gives us adequate instructions and we must either obey them or face a just God.

God Is a Just God

To be just, God must demand payment for sin. This applies to you and to me because each of us has sinned (Romans 3:23). What is the payment demanded for our sins? Death! (Romans 6:23) But a loving God takes no pleasure in our eternal destruction and is long-suffering, not wishing that anyone would perish (II Peter 3:9). But a just God must demand death for sin. Death unless a perfect sacrifice can be made for our sins! But none of us can serve as a perfect sacrifice because each of us has sinned. What a dilemma! Where would either man or God find such a perfect, sinless human? God alone knew the answer. He sent Jesus, His Son, without sin, who could serve as the perfect sacrifice to take away the guilt of sin and the sentence of eternal death. Thus, love and justice both were served.

To summarize, God is eternal, all-powerful, all-knowing, unchanging, dependable, loving, jealous, truthful, and just. Can we always say the same about all human beings?

THE NATURE OF MAN

Man was made in the image of God, but in man that image has become twisted, broken, and corroded. The image of God in man was first damaged by the sin of Adam and Eve in the Garden of Eden. And each succeeding generation has managed to do their share of damage to the image of God within themselves. But in our attempt to live the Christian life, we labor to straighten the twisted, to patch the broken, and to remove corrosion from the image of God that lives within us. In other words, we try to grow toward complete Christian maturity. Will we ever completely reach that commendable goal? To put it bluntly, NO! But, with God's help, we keep trying; and our humble, honest efforts, through Christ's blood, are made acceptable to God.

But what are these deformities that man has placed upon the image of God within him? We can't name them all here, but a study of the nature of man will, no doubt, reveal some of the sins man has used in his unintentional attempts to completely deface the image of God he has been so graciously given.

Man Is Not Uniformly Eternal

Man is a mixture of physical body which someday will die, and a spirit which is eternal. Physically speaking, if you shop in a variety store you will find in many instances boxes which cost more and probably are worth less than their contents. This is not true of humans. The container, the physical body, will someday disintegrate into dust; but the contents, the spirit, will live forever – someplace! And that is why Jesus rated the spirit far more valuable than any physical thing (Matthew 16:26), and why Jesus also pointed out that loss of the soul was far more devastating than merely the loss of physical life (Matthew 10:28). The physical body, we could say, serves as a transport to carry a person from birth to the grave. But the soul lives eternally. So you see, man is not uniform – he is a mixture of the perishable and the eternal.

And it is usually the perishable, or physical part of man that causes him trouble in this world and possibly in the world to come. Included in man's physical body are desires and drives which can trap him in sin, unless he seeks and obtains the help of a living God. Here are a few of the troublesome desires and drives for which we need God's help:

- ❖ Food, when used in the excess called "gluttony" (ouch!).
- ❖ Sex, not blessed by God in marriage vows (I Corinthians 7:2).
- ❖ Pleasure, when it prevents us from serving God (II Timothy 3:4).
- ❖ Popularity, when seeking it prevents us from serving God (Galatians 1:10).
- ❖ Covetousness, greed, wanting to accumulate things rather than serve God. Grumbling about the lack of things or willing to disobey God to get them. (We cannot serve God and Mammon. Matthew 6:24).
- ❖ Pride, (self-worship) unwillingness to humble oneself in obedience to God in repentance of sin, or in returning good for evil.

Working alone, man is not strong enough to overcome the drives and desires already mentioned and others not given here. Man is weak and must depend on God for help in escaping the temptations.

Man Is Not All-Powerful

The strongest of us are beset by many weaknesses. In the prime of life, we often find that our physical strength is too feeble for some tasks. And as the years pass, we find that more and more of our physical strength has left us. Spiritually this should not be so! In our prime, it is true that we may be too weak spiritually to escape some temptations; but as we grow older, our spiritual strength should increase, rather than decline. In other words, we should as time passes, be growing in strength spiritually. As we age, physically, we learn to depend more and more on power outside ourselves. Spiritually, too, we learn to depend more and more on God and fellow Christians for spiritual strength. And when old age comes we should have become a source of spiritual strength for our fellow Christians. This does not mean that we can count ourselves strong spiritually because out strength comes not from ourselves, but from the Lord. This is also true of wisdom.

Man Is Not All-Knowing
The statement that "man is not all-knowing," probably does not surprise you. Because of the explosion in knowledge in so many different fields, no one person can ever hope to learn everything. Instead, this is an age of specialization. To be successful in the complex physical world, we must set priorities on those areas of knowledge that we study. Spiritually, this statement is also true; and our number one priority should be learning more about God and His Word the Bible. A deep study of the Bible, followed by an equally careful practice of its concepts can make major changes in our lives.

Man Is Highly Changeable
Like the palm tree, man often bends with the wind for fear of being broken. A man who is your friend today may change into your enemy tomorrow, if it will help him to escape discomfort, danger, or other unpleasantness. Man who is a faithful Christian today, may have completely backslid by tomorrow, to our own amazement and to the amazement of the apostle Paul who wrote to the Christians

at Galatia: "I marvel that you are turning away so soon from Him who called you to the grace of Christ." Is being changeable good or bad? It can be either a curse or a blessing depending upon whether the change is made toward or away from the Lord. After all, each of us did change in becoming a Christian; and hopefully, we will continue to change by growing in the grace and knowledge of the Lord Jesus Christ. Such good change comes from prayer, Bible study and serving both God and our fellow man. Such regular service should show how dependable we are.

Man Is Not Always Dependable

What man says he will do, sometimes he cannot do. At other times, man is able to do what he said he would do and simply refuses to do it – with or without excuses. Each of us at times have been let down by a failure of someone to be where they said they would be or a failure to do what they promised. This does not mean that we should refuse to trust our fellow Christians to do what they agreed to do. But experience will prove who is and who is not dependable. By all means, unless circumstances prevent it, always honor your commitment – what you say you will do. Dependability is not only a characteristic of Boy Scouts, it is also a characteristic of a Christian – and it helps to build Christian love.

Man Is Not Always Loving

You probably didn't realize that man is sometimes unloving, did you? Of course you did! Each of us at times has endured some rather shabby treatment, thoughtless and cruel treatment, from our fellow men that are imperfect in love. How did it feel? Not good, huh? Well, as Christians, we must remember not to inflict pain on others. Remember the "Golden Rule". "Do unto others as you would have them do unto you" (Matthew 7:12). Is this always easy to do? No! But with God's help you can do it; and with prayer and Bible study you can grow in love to more closely resemble the love Jesus showed for us. And with this growth in love, you can overcome such sins as envy.

Man May be Either Jealous or Envious
"What is the difference between jealousy and envy?" you ask. Good question! Jealousy involves a RIGHT. For example, since God made us, He has the Right to expect our worship and when we worship something else, He has the RIGHT to be jealous. The same is true when a husband is jealous of another man who is a threat to his marriage. The husband has a RIGHT to be jealous; and such jealousy may help preserve a marriage – unless the husband loses control of himself. But with envy, we have a different situation: The person doing the envying has NO RIGHTS. Instead, a person who does not deserve or merit a thing, so strongly desires that thing that he resents the rightful owner or the person who actually deserves the reward or honor. Jealousy, if properly controlled, is desirable; envy is never acceptable and usually is based on the belief that the person doing the envying is more deserving than the rightful owner. This of course is not true.

Man Is Not Always Truthful
The very first lie was told by a serpent in the Garden of Eden. Not only did that lie get the serpent into trouble but it also caused trouble for Adam, Eve and the rest of us because that lie helped bring DEATH into the world. In fact, the seriousness of lying is shown by the Devil being called the Father of Liars (John 8:44). And since a man cannot have two fathers, an unrepentant liar cannot claim God as his father.

Of course, God is our father, and we as Christians would never tell a deliberate falsehood; but these are some more subtle forms of lying that a Christian should likewise avoid. For example, if we are not careful, we could be guilty of telling the truth but not the WHOLE truth. That statement would be a "half-truth", or if you prefer a "half lie". (To illustrate, let's say that Harry reported that John deliberately knocked down a five-year-old boy – a truth. But Harry failed to say that John did so to remove the boy from the path of an oncoming car. What damage could this "half truth" unfairly cause to John's reputation? Such half-truths are just as condemning to the one who tells them as are whole lies.)

And there is another type of lie that is also condemned by our Heavenly Father. This type is called flattery. What does God say about flattery? Proverbs 26:28 records that a flattering mouth works ruin," and in Proverbs 29:5 we find that a "man who flatters his neighbor spreads a net for his feet." But flattery also brings punishment to the one speaking such false words: As written in Psalms 12:2 and 3, "the Lord will cut off flattering lips."

We see then that any untruthful statement, whether whole lie, half lie, or flattery is condemned by God and should never be practiced by a Christian. God help us never to commit the injustice of lying about a person, place or thing.

Man Is Not Always Just

What causes a person to speak or act unjustly? There could be numerous reasons, but two of the most common are greed and envy. Because of greed, a person may make unfair statements or commit unfair acts in an effort to obtain something that he has no right to have. And because of envy, a person, resentful of another's good fortune or honor, may make unfair remarks about the more fortunate individual. Attacks by greedy or envious persons against other people, probably lead to recording of the ninth of the Ten Commandments, Which states: "Thou shalt not bear false witness against thy neighbor" (Exodus 20:16). And in Ephesians 4:15 we find recorded that we should "speak the truth in love." If we speak the truth in a loving way, we will not be guilty of making damaging and unjust statements because of greed or envy, and thereby adding one sin to another.

And at the time, it seems that we humans do just that – add on sin to another (hopefully repented of). However, to grow toward a less sinful life, we must depend upon God for the help He willingly provides in our relationship with Him.

THE RELATIONSHIP BETWEEN GOD AND MAN

In our discussion of the nature of God and Man, We have already stated, implied, or lead you to understand many of the relationships between God and man. Before reading this chapter, you probably were well acquainted with the existence of many of those relationships. If so, the chapter has served to reinforce what you already knew. Let us further reinforce your knowledge by giving the brief summary of some of the important relationships between God and Man. Here they are:

* ❖ Since God is eternal, we must be forever concerned about our relationship with Him.
* ❖ Since man's spirit is eternal and his physical body is not, man should give chief concern to spiritual things.
* ❖ Since God is all-powerful and we humans are not, we should rely less on our own strength and more on the strength that comes from God.
* ❖ Since God is all-knowing and we are not, we must learn to trust God for the direction of our lives. Only He can see the overall pattern of our complicated life.

❖ Since God is <u>unchanging</u>, we must learn to rely more and more upon His instructions and promises. Before we can rely on these words of God, however, we must first learn what they are. Bible study required!

❖ Since God is <u>loving</u>, we must appreciate what He does for us and what He allows to happen to us. Why? Because pleasant or unpleasant, God allows our experiences to promote our growth toward Christian maturity.

❖ Since God is a <u>jealous</u> God, we must grow in our love for Him and in our dependence upon Him. We must never delegate God to second place in our use of time, talents, money or other material possessions. At times, too, we may expect that humans will be envious of any success that we achieve, physically or spiritually. At such times, we must exercise self-control, must be kind, and must be forgiving in order to please God.

❖ Since God is <u>just</u>, we must be careful to avoid sinning, which could separate us from God. We must also expect that some people may be unjust toward us at times, and we must be able to respond in a Christian loving manner.

Now before we leave the relationship between God and man let's get a little more specific about this relationship. To do so, we discuss belief, love, glory, and pleasing in more detail.

Believe God First

Yes, we believe that God exists and that He rewards those who diligently seek Him (Hebrew 11:6). And we should believe that God is always right (Romans 3:4). If we do, when there is a disagreement between God and any man concerning what we should think, speak, or act, whom should we believe – God or man? In a case like this, the apostle Peter said that we should obey God rather than man (Acts 5:29)

Now, let me be so bold as to point out that you, too, are a man (or woman). This being true, when there is a disagreement between you and God on how you should act, whose opinion should decide the issue – yours or God's? Certainly God's opinion should rule because He is more reliable than any man. This is also true concerning the circumstances he sends your way. And there is another part in believing God: to believe that all things work together for your own good, whether those things are pleasant or unpleasant at the time (Romans 8:28). If we really love God as we should, such believing is not impossible for us.

Love God the Most

We should love God with all our heart, soul and mind (Matthew 22:37). Should we love our family, too? Yes, but not as much as we love the Lord (Matthew 10:37). How is our love for God shown? By our obedience of His commands (John 14:15). In case our family (or friend) wants us to do what they wish instead of doing what God wishes, what should a Christian do? Obey God, of course. We should try to please God rather than our families (Galatians 1:10). We should always remain faithful to God and glorify Him by our obedience to His commands.

Glorify God Only

The only thing a Christian should glory in is the Lord, his goodness and his power (I Corinthians 1:31). And to glory in the Lord should be done today, tomorrow, and forever (Galatians 1:5). We should glorify God in all walks of life and in everything we say and do (Colossians 3:17). And even as we do good deeds, we should see that God – not us- receives the credit (Matthew 5:16). Not only should we glorify God individually, but we should also glorify God in the Church (Ephesians 3:21).

So you see, a Christian should not glory (boast) in himself, which we sometimes do unintentionally when we say "I'll see you tomorrow!" But will we still be alive tomorrow? Only if God wills it to be so. Therefore we should say, "If the Lord wills, I will see you tomorrow!" (James 4: 13-16). This statement not only gives God the glory that He deserves, but also gives us a chance to influence other people by witnessing for the Lord. And it is pleasing to God!

Please God First
The fear of man contains a trap (Proverbs 29:25): It will lead us into sin. Jesus warns us not fear man but instead to fear God (Matthew 10:28). But perfect love (shown by perfect obedience to God's commands) casts out fear (I John 4:18). But such perfect obedience has been achieved only by Jesus.

Will you and I ever live up to the high standard of obedience shown by Jesus? Probably not! But to be pleasing to God we must give it our best effort and then confess our failures and repent of them. Your conscientious efforts in doing will be well-pleasing to God, when coupled with Christ's blood.

But remember this: with all our heart, we must try not to commit sin, because if we do sin, Satan is our master; and we are his slaves (Romans 6:16). As Christians, however, we should be a slave to God not to sin and Satan. What is sin? It is the failure to obey God's commands. Sin is unrighteousness, for all of God's commands are righteous (Psalms 119:172). So we must strive with all our heart to avoid sin, even the sin that results from leaving undone the things we know that we should do (James 4:17). To please God we must do good to all men (Galatians 6: 10).

42

So much for our discussion for the nature of man, the nature of God, and the relationship between man and God. Now, let's review what we covered by completing the following exercises, titled "Let's See What You've Learned."

After completing these exercises, please complete the additional exercise, titled "Now Let's Get Personal."

<u>Section II: Let's See What You've Learned</u>

1. The reason we should study the nature of God and the nature of man is to

   _____

   _____

2. Why can't we understand the nature of God completely?_____

   _____

3. Why is it important to us humans that God is eternal?_____

   _____

4. What are some evidences that God is all-powerful?_____

   _____

5. Why does God know us so well?

   _____

   _____

6. Why is it important that God is unchanging?

    _____

    _____

7. What do we mean by the statement that God is

    dependable?_____

    _____

8. How has God shown his love for us?

    _____

    _____

    _____

9. What do we mean by the term "tough love"?

    _____

    _____

10. We know that God is a jealous God because

    it is stated in _____ _____.

11. What causes God to be jealous?

    _____

    _____

12. What things besides graven images can also

    serve as idols? _____

    _____

    _____

13. What does it mean to "tell the WHOLE truth"? _____

_____

_____

14. What does it mean: "God is a just God"?

_____

_____

15. How can a just God keep from pronouncing the sentence of death on each of us sinners?

_____

_____

16. Why is the Spirit of man not a perfect image of God? _____

_____

_____

17. What pattern can we use in trying to change the spirit of man into the pure image of God?

_____

_____

_____

(John 14:8; I Corinthians 11:1)

18. Explain the statement: "Man is only Partly eternal"_____

_____

_____

19. What are some of the desires and drives that may draw us away from God?

_____

_____

_____

20. In what sense should a man grow stronger instead of weaker as he ages and becomes old? _____

_____

21. Since we cannot learn everything in this complex and confusing world, what learning should take # 1 priority? _____ And Why?

_____

_____

_____

_____

22. Man is highly changeable. Is this good or bad? _____

_____

23. Why would you classify the "Golden Rule" as the rule of love? _____

_____

_____

24. Explain: envy itself is a sin which can lead to what other types of sin? _____

_____

_____

25. Why can't an <u>unrepentant</u> liar be called a child of God? _____

_____

_____

26. What is meant by the term "half truth"?

_____

_____

_____

27. Why is flattery condemned in the Bible?

_____

_____

_____

28. Which of the Ten Commandments covers unjust remarks made by and envious person?

_____

_____

29. What is the only source of pure truth in all the books of the world?_____

_____

_____

30. As a Christian, what sources of helpful strength are available to us?

_____

_____

31. In case of conflict between what God says and what our family says, Whom should we believe and why? _____

_____

_____

32. If I plan to see you tomorrow, what can I say to give God the glory and to give me a chance to influence other people for God?

_____

_____

_____

33. What should I do instead of bragging about the good works I have done? What would you say to accomplish this? _____

_____

_____

34. How do we prove that our love for the Lord is

real? _____

_____

_____

Section III: Now, Let's Get Personal

A. In the list below, place a plus (+) before each number preceding an item for which you feel that you do NOT need considerable improvement.

B. Then place a circle around five of the number preceding an item in which you believe you need the greatest improvement. This is your priority #1 list.

C. And finally, place a minus (-) before each number preceding an item needing improvement, but with a #2 priority.

D. Begin an active program of self-improvement, concentrating first on the circle numbered items and later on the items with a minus sign.

E. Before you start the program, however, and before each day of the program, pray for the Lord to help you. Amen

1. Placing spiritual things ahead of material things.
2. Freedom from gluttony (overeating).
3. Freedom from sex outside of marriage.
4. Putting service to God ahead of pleasure.
5. Putting service to God ahead of popularity.
6. Freedom from covetousness (greed).
7. Giving thanks to God instead of grumbling.
8. Humbly submitting to the will of God.
9. Quick to confess faults and repent of sins.
10. Willingly return good for evil.
11. Learning to lean more and more upon God.

12. Giving Bible Study Priority (daily study).
13. Eager to change when I see that I have sinned or am mistaken.
14. Striving to grow in the grace and knowledge of Christ.
15. Dependable: I do what I say I will do, Always.
16. Growing in the ability to follow the "Golden Rule"
17. Learning to overcome envy without committing other sins.
18. Careful to tell the truth and the WHOLE truth.
19. Learning to give honest compliments without flattery.
20. Learning to speak the truth in a loving way.
21. Learning to trust God to direct my life.

Chapter III. YOUR NEW RELATIONSHIP WITH GOD'S BLESSINGS,

Section 1: Let's Talk About It.

"Know ye that the Lord He is God...enter into His gates with thanksgiving and into His courts with praise; be thankful unto Him and bless His name." (Psalm 100:3, 4)

Have you ever spent a great deal of thought trying to decide on exactly the right gift for a friend? And then, of course, there was the frustration of going from store to store until finally you found the desired gift. And how your spirit soared when your friend profusely thanked you and in other ways showed his hearty approval and deep appreciation for your gift!

But suppose the look on your friend's face had clearly shown that he did not really appreciate your gift; that he failed to thank you, and that he even openly criticized your gift? How would you have felt? I wonder if God does not feel the same way when we accept His abundant blessings, take them for granted, fail to thank Him, and even bemoan the fact that He has not given us more.

Is God hurt by such lack of appreciation? I know that Jesus was hurt, as given in the 17th chapter of Luke. There it is recorded that Jesus cured ten men of leprosy but that only one man returned to thank Jesus. Jesus then said, "Were not ten cleansed? But where are the nine?" How disappointed and stung Jesus must have felt at this lack of appreciation. And remember, Jesus said, "...he that has seen me hath seen the Father" (John 14:9). So I conclude that God is also stung by our ingratitude for His many rich gifts.

Many of God's gifts are given to every human, whether or not they are Christians. Other, more rich gifts, are reserved only for God's Children. Let's first discuss the gifts common to all men. But even where such common gifts are concerned we Christians should be deeply thankful.

GIFTS COMMON TO ALL MEN

It would not be practical here to list all the gifts that God has given to all men: It would indeed be a long catalogue. But there are several gifts so rich that they certainly should be mentioned here, particularly since they are the ones we most often take for granted. These important but so often unappreciated gifts include the human body, air, and water.

The Marvelous Human Body

Recently, a machine was invented that could diagnose its own troubles and even make some of the minor needed repairs. "Remarkable!" you say, "A marvel of modern engineering." But our Heavenly Father invented such a machine with even better features at least 7,000 years ago. We call the machine the human body, and it is indeed a marvelous creation. Let's look at some of its amazing features, beginning with a simple one, – or is it? – the human thumb.

❖ The human hand boast a thumb, a member of the hand that really makes man physically superior to nearly all animals and makes civilization possible. (Try holding a hammer or an eggbeater without using your thumb.)

❖ The brain with billions of cells so marvelously connected that it makes possible many complex functions.

❖ Automatic control for body heat, a super thermostat that perfectly controls body temperature without giving trouble for 70 years or more. Where else can you find such quality equipment?

❖ An automatic override for the thermostat to raise body temperature above normal when it becomes necessary to fight a disease or an infection.

❖ An automatic control that regulates breathing frequency to supply needed oxygen for the body. (What a boresome and wasteful process it would be if we had to consciously say, "Inhale, exhale, inhale, exhale" in order to breath correctly.")

❖ An automatic system to control digestion of foods. If we had to personally control digestion, we would be in a heap of trouble, since we would need to personally control:
1. The flow of saliva to the mouth.
2. The swallowing action of the mouth.
3. The rippling action of the esophagus.
4. The churning action of the stomach.
5. The action of the pyloric valve.
6. The action of millions of villa in the small intestine.
7. The dehydrating and conveying actions of the large intestines.

❖ An automatic alarm system that responds to emergencies by sending a surge of adrenalin into the blood to strengthen the action of the body.

❖ An automatic short-circuit action that, for example, withdraws a hand from a hot stove before the hand can burn and before the brain has time to signal such a withdrawal.

What a wonderful, wonderful body the dear Lord has given us – and before we leave our discussion of this marvelous machine – let's also be thankful for the blessing of <u>pain</u>. What did you say? Thankful for pain? Yes! Without the feeling of pain, we might stand on flaming wood until our feet burned off. But pain sends a sharp warning so that the feet can be saved. This is an extreme example, of course, but I believe you get the point. Thank the Lord, <u>even for pain.</u> And be thankful, too, for another simple but important blessing – the air we breathe.

The Marvelous Air We Breathe

The God Lord really was careful with his recipe for air: 23% oxygen, 76% nitrogen and a 1% mixture of carbon dioxide, hydrogen, helium and other trace gases. If the oxygen content was greatly reduced, we humans would die; and if the oxygen content was greatly increased, the world would probably burn up. Too much carbon dioxide and we would suffocate. Too much hydrogen and the world would explode if there was even a small spark. And too much helium to breathe and we would all talk like chipmunks. And what good does nitrogen do? During a thunderstorm, when lightening strikes, the electrical charge and nitrogen combine to make the world's most perfect fertilizer – and just watch those crops grow! Thank you Lord for your great recipe for air, even if man sometimes does smog it up!

Man, too, sometimes pollutes another of God's great blessings – water.

The Marvelous Water We Use

And water is so widely used by man. First of all, man's body is over 60% water, and water enters nearly every function of the body in one form or another. Without water, crops die, and fish become highly embarrassed. Without water humans soon die. Without water, firefighting would be nearly impossible and very expensive. And without water, our cleaning bills would certainly become huge. Water is so widely used that it has been correctly called the "universal solvent."

Water, however, is remarkable in another aspect: it's peculiar reaction to temperature changes. As the temperature falls, as you would suspect, water shrinks in size until it reaches 34 degrees F. Then – surprise, surprise

– as temperature continues to drop below 34 degrees F., water <u>expands</u> in size, therefore becoming lighter in weight so that ice is lighter than water and will float. Is that important? Yes! If this were not true, the ice being heavier than water would sink to the bottom, carrying fish and other marine life with it. What a mess that would be: all the fish frozen in ice at the bottom of the water. Thank God for his careful engineering.

Now, before we leave the blessings common to all men, let's make honorable mention of a few additional other.

Other Blessings Common to All Men

Here, though not discussed in great detail, are the following additional blessings common to all men.

- ❖ The amazing physical laws composed by God which keep Mother Earth contentedly holding its assigned place in the solar system.

- ❖ The constancy of Earth's gravity that insures that an object dropped will fall <u>down</u> rather than <u>up</u> or <u>sideways</u>. (Don't laugh at this blessing. Just ask our astronauts.)

- ❖ The blessing of work that lessens the amount of trouble we get into. (Idleness is the Devil's workshop!) And I believe that God meant for work to be a blessing for man when God said, "Cursed is the ground for thy sake...In the sweat of thy face thou shalt eat bread."

- ❖ The Holy Bible, God's Word, that, when effectively studied can lead man to an obedient, saving faith in the Lord Jesus.

- ❖ The food, clothing and shelter which we enjoy and which some non-Christians claim that they earned exclusively by their own work and therefore do not need to be thankful to God. (How did they "earn" their body, the air, the

55

water and other things that make their work possible?)

❖ The blessing of family and friends which is also a gift (or rather a <u>loan</u>) from God to make our lives more enjoyable and worthwhile.

Oh! How grateful we should be even for the blessings common to all men, but we should be even more thankful for the spiritual blessings reserved especially for us Christians.

GIFTS RESERVED FOR CHRISTIANS

As you will recall the gifts common to all men are mainly of a physical nature; but the gifts reserved for Christians are principally of a spiritual nature. Actually, each of these spiritual blessings comes from a joint effort of God, Jesus, and the Holy Spirit, working together. But to simplify our discussions, let's just say that each of these gifts comes principally from one of the Holy Three, beginning with those which come from Jesus.

Spiritual Blessings from Jesus

Perhaps some of the richest gifts of love are shown not by what we give but by what we personally give up – a sacrifice. And Jesus gave up many things to show His love for us and to bring us spiritual blessings. Are we always aware of the sacrifices he made? It's easy to remember His willing death upon the cross as a great sacrifice for our benefit. But Jesus' sacrifices began long before the cross. For example, His first sacrifice – and it was a great one – was leaving the riches and glory of heaven and emptying Himself of his equality with God (Philippians 2: 1-9).

Then, too, He gave up a glorious spiritual body for a heavenly body with all its temptations, aches, pain, and tiredness. (Think of how aching with tiredness He must have been after walking many miles to bring healing and

56

the gospel to those people who sorely needed such help.) How much unselfishness He showed in order to <u>live and example</u> for you and for me – a great sacrifice and a great gift!

Humility
Think, too, of how much <u>humiliation</u> He bore for you and me as He was regularly, publicly <u>contradicted</u> in His teaching, accused of being the son of the devil, falsely accused at a mock trial, slapped contrary to the law, spit upon, stripped naked and mocked in public, and ridiculed as He hung on the cross. Yet He withstood all of this and <u>forgave</u> His tormentors in order to set an example of godly living for you and for me. Not only did Jesus lay down his <u>life</u> for us on the cross but He also laid down His <u>living</u> for us before, and during His crucifixion. And such a godly example should make it easy for you and for me to forgive those who have sinned against us. And that brings us to our first spiritual blessing to be discussed: forgiveness.

Forgiveness
Christ's blood is the "wonder drug." We were infected with sin and had no way to overcome this "cancer" that was slowly but surely eating away our spiritual life. Then Christ's blood was made available to those with an obedient faith who wished to be cured of this life-threatening "tumor." This "wonder drug" not only removed the tumor (guilt of sin) but also gave us power to guard against relapse. Weak as we humans are, however, from time to time, try as we may, we still stumble. So Jesus makes available a small does of the miracle drug (His blood) which sprinkles away the guilt of our sins so long as we are honestly trying to obey Jesus (I john 1:7). But here's a word of warning: Like Jesus we must forgive those who sin against us. Otherwise, the "wonder drug" won't work for us: We will still be guilty of ALL our sins

57

(Matthew 6: 14-15). Lord, we pray that this will never happen to any of us.

Prayer
Another rich blessing that Jesus brought to us is the right to pray in His name. Praying in Jesus' name means to pray for things Jesus would approve of or authorize. (To pray in His name is to pray according to His authority.) When we pray using the name of Jesus and ask for things which please him, God will hear and will answer our prayers (John 14: 13-14). One important thing to pray for regularly is for God to grant us wisdom to help us to understand the Bible (James 1:5). A clear understanding will help us to avoid sinning. But try as we may, at times we may stumble into sin; and for such "crimes" we will need a good lawyer to plead our case before our Heavenly Father.

Pleading Our Case If we do sin, we have an advocate (lawyer) to plead our case: Jesus Christ the righteous (I John 2:1). Since our lawyer, Jesus, has been tempted in all ways just as we have been tempted (Hebrews 4:15), He understands us and is equipped to plead for us and to apply His blood to wash away our sins: Verdict: NOT GUILTY! Since we all sin, how comforting it is to know that we have such a skilled lawyer representing us in the court of Heaven. And Jesus' fees are reasonable too: our earnest effort for complete obedience of God's commands.

As I already pointed out, the spiritual blessings which come from Jesus include forgiveness of sins, pleading our case in heaven, and help in our prayers. Other help in our prayers comes from the Holy Spirit.

Spiritual Blessings from the Holy Spirit

Not only does the Holy Spirit help us in praying but he also helps us in Bible Study, helps to activate our conscience, and grants us the fruits of the Spirit. Let's briefly discuss each of these blessings.

The Holy Spirit's Help in Prayer

How does the Holy Spirit help our prayers? Sometimes we feel a need so strongly that we cannot seem to put it into appropriate words in our prayers. The Holy Spirit then takes over and translates our feelings into acceptable words (Romans 8:26). And the Holy Spirit is also helpful in bringing to us other acceptable words, those found in the Bible.

The Holy Spirit's Help with the Bible

After Christ ascended into heaven, the Holy Spirit brought to the apostles' remembrance the teaching given by Christ while here on earth (John 14:26). Not only that, but the Holy Spirit guided the apostles in all truth. So we see that the Bible came to us in a complete, correct, and truthful form. How thankful should we be for the perfect Word of God? Very thankful, because we know that we can completely depend upon the Bible in a world otherwise filled with lack of certainty. Since we know that we can depend upon the Bible's accuracy, we should study all parts of it, whether simple or hard to understand. In chapter four of this book, we will have a great deal more to say about the use of the Bible.

Here, however, let us point out that a study of the Bible helps to train our conscience and to sensitize it to the work of the Holy Spirit in activating our conscience.

The Holy Spirit's Help with Our Conscience

How close is the Holy Spirit to you? -- One mile away, 100 yards, or even closer? Since you have become a

Christian, the Holy Spirit lives within you (I Corinthians 3: 16), and that's pretty close, isn't it? So the Holy Spirit is always there willing to help you if you will but let him. How does he help you where your conscience is concerned? Well, he brought the Bible to help train your conscience. That's one way he helps. And I believe that he works with God to activate a spiritual alarm, sending an aching, throbbing pain to our conscience when we realize that we have done wrong.

But is the conscience a reliable guide? Yes and No! If your conscience says, "No! Don't do it. It's wrong!" Believe your conscience because "...if your own conscience condemn us, God is greater than our conscience and knows all things" (I John 3:20). And if your conscience says, "It may be alright but, I have my doubts." Don't do it because "...he that doubteth is damned if he eats because he eateth not in faith: for whatsoever is not of faith is sin" (Romans 14:23). But if your conscience says, "Oh! I believe it will be alright," don't assume that your conscience is being truthful: Check it out! Study the Bible and talk with Christians who may be older in the faith than you. To ask and "older" brother for help is very pleasing to him.

So carefully notice what your conscience says. When it speaks to you, you are receiving one of the blessings of the Holy Spirit, which generously gives us many fruits of the Spirit.

The Holy Spirit gives us many Rich Fruits

What rich fruits are given to you by the Holy Spirit? They include love, joy, peace, long-suffering, gentleness, goodness, faith, meekness, and temperance. Let's briefly discuss each of these gifts.

Love

The two greatest commandments in the Bible are to love God and to love your fellow man (Matthew 22:36-39). Jesus further emphasized the importance of love by saying that people can recognize that we are disciples by our love for one another (John 13:35). And we know that God is love (I John 4:8) and that love comes from God (I John 4:7). In a sense then we are but mirrors that reflect God's love to the world – unless our mirrors get clouded over with sin, much like a bathroom mirror is clouded with steam during a hot shower.

But what kind of love are we talking about? Not sexual love for the unmarried: that's called "fornication," it's sinful; and we are warned to flee from it (I Corinthians 6:18). No! We are talking about a holy type of love called "agape love' a love that seeks the highest good of a person, a love that motivates other people to love and good works (Hebrews 10:24). And such a love is shown to us by our Heavenly Father who expects us to reflect that love to a world that is sadly in need of it. Such a love brings a joy that is lasting to both the giver and the receiver.

Joy

A heart that is fouled by the unwholesome feelings of envy or hate has no room for joy. Such a heart is the Devil's workshop, soon leading to other sins. But Jesus teaches us to have a forgiving heart, to purge out the old sinful feelings, thus to draw nearer to God and to experience the contentment and joy that only the Lord can give. Such feelings lead the Christian to daily rejoicing because we are God's favored Children (Philippians 4:4). And with such rejoicing comes a feeling of great peace.

Peace

Jesus said, "My peace I leave you" (John 14:27). But what kind of peace did Jesus have? He was cursed, beaten, and crucified! How peaceful does that sound?

Jesus was not talking about peace with the world. In fact, Christians are told "He who would live a godly life in Christ Jesus _will_ suffer persecution" (II Timothy 3:12). No! Jesus was not talking about peace with the world. But instead he was talking about peace with God, the kind of peace we feel when we know that we have God's love and that we have done God's will. With this knowledge comes the peace that passeth all understanding (Philippians 4:1-7). God's peace, closeness, and approval comes to those who have suffered long for His sake.

Longsuffering

"Be not weary in well doing, for in due season we shall reap if we faint not" (Galatians 6:9). Patience – keeping on keeping on – is one of the Christian virtues. Even if there are rocks in the furrows we will eventually reach the desired goal if we keep plowing. Never give up, if the objective is worth achieving. Be careful, however, not to become so discouraged that you lose self-control. Such a sin would be disastrous if you were trying to persuade a friend to become a Christian. With such a worthwhile goal, make certain that what you do and say are all done in a spirit of gentleness.

Gentleness

The apostle Paul, in describing his treatment of the brethren at Thessalonica, said that he treated them as gentle as a mother nursing her baby. And that is how gentle we should treat a friend that we are trying to lead to Christ. At this time, your friend no doubt feels a little alarmed, besieged, and ready at any harsh sound to flee like a bird to the mountains. Gentleness is a must if we are to succeed as Christians. And another must is goodness.

Goodness

The apostle Paul states that a person would probably not sacrifice his life for a righteous man but that he might do so for a good man (Romans 5:7). But what's the difference between a righteous man and a good man? A righteous man is one who obeys every letter of the law; he would give you exactly what is required, no more and no less. A good man, however, is one who will give you better treatment than you deserve. For example, during the "Great Depression" when money was scarce, a neighborhood grocer was a good man (by chance, named Mr. Christian). He knew that there were eleven members in our family so he gave us eleven slices of bologna no matter how much money we sent him - 25 cents, 30 cents, or 40 cents. He gave us better treatment than we deserved. We have all sinned but God sent His Son to pay for our sins, showing how good He was by giving us better treatment than we deserved. Go thou and do likewise to your fellow man. This requires that you be a meek person.

Meekness

Meekness is not a weakness. It is strength under control. A bit in the horse's mouth keeps the beast's tremendous strength under control. Similarly, meekness allows a person to keep all his powers under control. For example, Christ had power to call down about twelve legions of angels (about 6,000) to take Him off the cross, but He did not do so. Otherwise there would be no sacrifice and no forgiveness for our sins. With His meekness, Christ kept His awesome power in check and allowed Himself to do what was best, even laying down His life for you and me. When the test comes for you and for me, will we display such Christ-like meekness? Lord, we pray that we will. Help us Lord to display self-control in our relationship with other people and help us to show temperance where the use of things is concerned.

Temperance

During the days of prohibition of alcoholic beverages, the word "temperance" meant to leave alcoholic beverages alone. Now, however, the word "temperance" has a much broader meaning. It now means to make the right use of things, to place our will under the controlling power of the spirit of God. If this is done, the key word seems to be "moderation." Eat food, but only what is actually needed – no gluttony; and also moderation in all we say and do. Never say or do anything to excess, but keep our use within the limits set by reason, no by emotion or physical desires. This must be done if we are to walk in the light – the truth of God.

Truth

There are two distinct meanings of the word truth. First, there is eternal truth, the Word of God. And certainly the Holy Spirit brought this Truth into the world to help us know how to live. And second, the word "truth" means to tell what is accurate, not a lie. If we tell a lie, the Holy Spirit helps by giving us an aching conscience and thus encourages us always to be truthful. But God is also helpful in giving us an aching conscience.

Spiritual Blessings from God.

Of course, God helps to bring us each of the blessings we have already discussed. But two blessings should be more thoroughly covered here: chastisement and trials. Chastisements activate the pain (nerve) system of our spiritual life: they cause a throbbing ache when we know that we have done wrong. Chastisements may come directly from God, as is true when our conscience pains us; or chastisements maybe sent by God through other people in order to lead us to depend more upon Him and to lead us to repent of our misdeeds.

But regardless of how God administers the "spanking," we should be grateful for it, because it is intended to save our spiritual life. Then too, the chastisement proves that God still loves us and still considers us to be His children (Hebrews 12:5-7). Thus we humbly bow to God during chastisement and as we meet and conquer trials and temptations, we grow as Christians and become more closely molded toward the image of the Lord Jesus.

That concludes our discussion of the physical and spiritual blessings that come from Jesus, the Holy Spirit, and God. To see what you have learned, answer the following exercises:

<u>Section II: Let's See What You've Learned</u>

1. I know that Jesus felt hurt by the lack of appreciation

   because _____

   _____

   (Luke 17:12-17)

2. What do you think is the most remarkable thing about

   the   human   body   God   gave   us?

   _____

   _____

   _____

3. Why was God's recipe for air so important?

   _____

   _____

4. In what way is the water God made so unique?

   _____

_____

_____

5. How would you answer a person who claimed: "I don't
   need to thank God for food, clothing, and shelter
   because I worked to earn these things myself?

   _____

   _____

6. When does Christ' blood first cover our sins?

   _____

   _____

7. What does it mean to pray in the name of Christ?

   _____

   _____

8. Now that Christ is in heaven, what things does He now
   do for us Christians where sin is concerned?

   _____

   _____

   _____

9. How does the Holy Spirit help us in prayer?

   _____

_____

_____

10. How does the Holy Spirit help us where the Bible is concerned? _____

_____

_____

11. When   is   the   conscience   a   reliable   guide?

_____

_____

_____

12. When   is   the   conscience   not   a   reliable   guide?
_____ and   what   should   be
done in that case?_____

_____

_____

13. What   are   the   fruits   of   the   Holy   Spirit?

_____

_____

_____

14. What   are   the   two   greatest   commandments?
_____ and

_____

15. How can people tell that we are Christ's disciples?

_____

_____

_____

16. What kind of love is intended in question 14 and 15?

_____

_____

17. Why should a Christian's heart be filled with joy?

_____

_____

18. What kind of peace did Jesus leave us?

_____

_____

19. How gentle was Paul in talking to fellow Christians?

_____

_____

_____

20. What is the difference between a righteous man and a good man? _____

_____

_____

21. What does the word meekness mean?

_____

_____

22. What does the word temperance mean as used in the Bible? _____

_____

_____

23. In what two ways does the Holy Spirit help us where truth is concerned? _____

_____

_____

24. In what two ways does God help us to develop as Christians? _____

_____

_____and

_____

_____

Section III: Now Let's Get Personal

1. Use the following rating system on each of the items listed below: 1. Failing: 2. Poor: 3. Marginal: 4. Average: 5. Good
2. List each item rated 1 or 2 on the lines below the rating items and tells how you plan to make the needed improvements.
   a. Do I really appreciate what God has done for me?
   b. Do I show appreciation for my marvelous human body by taking care of it?
   c. Do I really appreciate the air I breathe?
   d. Do I really appreciate God for the unique features of water?
   e. Do I really appreciate God for the loan of family members to me?

f. Have you made sacrifices for the Lord?
g. Are you willing to stand humiliation for the Lord?
h. Will you pray only for the things which would please Jesus?
i. Do you always try to obey Jesus?
j. Do you seek the Holy Spirit's help in your Bible study?
k. Are you able to tell a friend, chapter and verse, on how to be saved?
l. Do you rely too much on your conscience for guidance?
m. Do you try to encourage others to love and good works?
n. Are you always gentle in your treatment of others?
o. Do you always try to give other people better treatment that they deserve?
p. Are you meek? Do you have your power under control?
q. Do you show moderation in your eating and sleeping?
r. Do you always tell the truth?
s. Are you truly grateful for your chastisements from God?

1. _____

_____

_____

_____

2. _____

_____

George J. Cunningham, Sr.

3. _____

_____

_____

4. _____

_____

_____

5. _____

_____

_____

Chapter IV. YOUR NEW RELATIONSHIP WITH GOD'S WORD

Section 1: Let's Talk About It.

Esau was of all men most fortunate – at least at first. As the oldest son of a very wealthy man, he was entitled to the oldest son's birthright – a double share of the estate. He was also fortunate in another way: he loved to hunt wild game and his father willingly let him do so. But one day after a long period of hunting, he was nearly famished and his physical desire led him to make a poor bargain with his brother Jacob. Esau traded Jacob his birthright for a bowl of beans. That's about ten cents worth of beans in exchange for property worth many thousands of dollars, simply because he could not control his physical desire. Not a very good bargain for Esau, was it?

We as Christians would never be guilty of such a poor bargain: letting a physical desire cost us such a fortune; would we? Don't be too sure! Would we ever be guilty of letting a physical desire for food, sex, pleasure, popularity, or material things cost us a bigger fortune than Esau lost – our home in heaven? "No!" you say, "we would never sell our home in heaven for such comparatively worthless things." But what if you unknowingly violate some of God's laws because you have not studied long enough or thoroughly enough to learn those laws? Looking at Luke 12:48,49, we see that a servant will be punished for disobeying the Master's law even though that servant did not know that law. *Ignorance of the law is no excuse.*

And Jesus has said, "If you love me, you will keep my commandments (John 14:15). But how can we be sure we are keeping Christ's commandments if we do not know those commandments? If we do not care enough for Christ to learn His commandments, how can we say that we love him?

Now, please allow me to make another approach to the subject of Bible study by means of the avenue of politeness. Have you ever met a "conversational hog", one who demanded to do all of the talking and none of the listening? Such rudeness is rather frustrating and disgusting, isn't it? Well, if we pray regularly to God but do not listen to Him in Bible study at home and in class, have we not become a "conversational hog" where God is concerned? Our conversation with God should include prayer (talking) and Bible study (listening). So let's keep our conversation polite: Let's pray daily and daily study the Bible. By doing so, we might earn God's rating of "noble". How can you and I earn a "noble" rating from God? It's not too difficult to achieve if we set our minds to it. God's word tells us how when it states about the people of Berea: "These were more noble than those of Thessalonica [why Lord] because they received the word will all readiness of mind and searched the scriptures daily, to see whether these things were so." (Acts 17:11) Did you notice the two requirements?

1. Receive the word with readiness – be motivated and prepared by prayer and study before coming to Bible class. And study the Bible at all possible opportunities.

2. Search the scriptures daily to see if the things taught are so. *Have you noticed the many scripture references in this book to help you check my teaching?* I would never deliberately mislead you, but anyone—preacher, teacher, elder or deacon—can be honestly mistaken; and the salvation of our souls is too important to just guess about. So check out this teacher, check out every teacher. Remember to study the Bible daily and check all teaching for accuracy. By

doing so you can win a blue ribbon—God's rating of "noble."

By now, you may think that I believe Bible study is important to the life of a Christian. Well! You are right! Without the comfort, instruction, and motivation of the Bible, we would be stumbling around without strength in a sad and evil world, a world that demands that Christians have a great spiritual strength. Don't try to make it without the help of the Bible, my friend.

In summary, we should study the Bible to keep ourselves safe in the arms of Jesus, to show our love for Jesus, to show politeness in our conversation with God, and to earn God's rating of "noble."

In your quest of a "noble" rating, you may read some Bible verses that you do not understand. We all have this trouble to a greater or lesser degree. But don't be discouraged. Each of us has to grow in our ability to understand the Bible; and to help you do this we will discuss the following subjects in this chapter:

- ❖ How the Bible should serve you.
- ❖ Preparing for Bible study.
- ❖ Tips for Bible study.
- ❖ Parts of the Bible to study.
- ❖ Resources that help us understand the Bible.

HOW SHOULD THE BIBLE SERVE YOU?

The Bible should serve you by acting as a magnet, a mirror, a source of wisdom, a motivator, and a diamond mine. Since this statement may seem a bit puzzling to you, perhaps I should explain.

The Bible Is A Magnet
When we study the Bible, we will be impressed by the beautiful nature of Jesus—His helpful unselfish life, his amazing self-control, and the death he died for you and me.

When viewing such a wonderful life, we cannot help but be drawn to Him like iron to a magnet. And we cannot help but grow in our love for Jesus. *How great is your love for Jesus now?* A poem located in the back of the book (page A-1) should help you measure your love, using the acid test of obedience (John 14:15). The poem may also help you set some goals for your growth as a Christian. Yes! The Bible is a magnet that draws us closer to the Lord, but the Bible is also a mirror.

The Bible Is A Mirror
The poet Wee Bobby Burns said, among other things: "Would some gift the giftie give us to see ourselves as others see us." Well, no one has given us that gift yet; however, we do have a mirror to see how we are doing spiritually—the Bible. But immediately please allow me to point out that we now see only darkly as in that mirror (I Corinthians 13:12). In Bible times mirror were made of polished metal which, at best, gave only a blurred reflection. And a loving Heavenly Father allows us to see our spiritual condition only darkly. If we clearly saw all our sins, flaws and weakness at once, we would be so discouraged that we would not try to grow as a Christian. So, like a good parent, God, little by little, reveals to us our defects as we grow stronger and better able to withstand correction. And how does He reveal to us our need to improve—through Bible reading and Bible class, which make us wiser.

The Bible Is A Source of Wisdom
There is an old saying that "fools rush in where angels dare not tread." In effect this proverb is saying that lack of wisdom endangers our lives, both physically and spiritually. To see this is so, lets first see what the characteristics of Christian wisdom are. The wisdom from above is "pure, peaceable, gentle, easy to be entreated,

76

merciful, impartial, and without hypocrisy (James 3:17). If we lack these characteristics, we can create trouble that can even lead to our death. "How can that be," you ask? Well, suppose that a person is living an impure life by committing adultery with another man's wife. The <u>Bible</u> warns us that "jealousy is the rage of man; therefore he will not spare in the day of vengeance"(Proverbs 6:34). Or suppose that you have spread a false rumor about a man. We are also warned: "What man is he desires life and loves many days that he may see good? Keep thy tongue from evil and thy lips from speaking guile (Psalms 34:12,13). These are but two of many <u>Bible</u> teachings that could add to our wisdom.

Now, before we leave our discussion of the wisdom given to us by the <u>Bible</u> let us point out that Jesus is the wisdom of God (I Corinthians 1:24). To see if this is true, let's ask ourselves, "Is Christ pure, peaceable, gentle, easy to be entreated, merciful, impartial, and without hypocrisy?" Obviously, the answer is "Yes!" And since we Christians should imitate Christ, we should be motivated to develop these characteristics in our own lives.

The Bible Is A Motivator

There are four types of motivation: The internal motivators of love and hate, and the external motivators of rewards or punishments. The Bible encourages the internal motivation of love but condemns the internal motivation of hate (Matthew 22: 37-39; Matthew 5:43,44). The <u>Bible</u> promises the external motivation of heaven and a crown of life for those who obey Jesus (Hebrews 5:9). The <u>Bible</u> also promises the external motivation of dishonor and damnation in a Devil's hell for those who refuse to obey Jesus (II Peter 2:9). The Bible, then, has many shining gems of motivation.

The Bible Is A Diamond Mine

Near the northwest corner of Arkansas, a traveler may see signs advertising a field where a person may search to find and to keep small diamonds. In many instances, these precious stones may easily be gathered from the top of the ground until all have disappeared. With the passing of time, however, the wind and the rain remove more of the topsoil and expose more easy-to-find diamonds. But to find the largest and most beautiful diamonds, a person must dig, dig and dig still deeper.

And that pretty well describes our experience in Bible study. Many bright shining gems of the Bible adorn the surface, there for easy picking. Other beautiful gems await the passing of time as the winds and rains of our experience expose them to our understanding. Still other gems, the most beautiful of all, require that we earnestly dig, dig, dig to uncover the message God intends for us to have. Such hard works require preparation if we are to be successful.

But before we talk about such preparation, lets discuss a few other facts that may be helpful to you if you are serious in your desire to grow in the Lord.

As stated before, some parts of the Bible contain beautiful gems that are easy to discover. The prophet Isaiah wrote about such easy-to-find diamonds when he pointed out:

> "And a highway shall be called the way of holiness...the wayfaring men, though fools, shall not err therein." (Isaiah 35:8)

Examples of such simple, easy-to-understand teachings are those which point out our path to salvation. These include:

78

❖ Hear the Word of God
   (Romans 10:17)
❖ Believe that God is and that He rewards
   those who diligently seek Him (Hebrews
   11:6)
❖ Confess your faith in Christ before men.
   (Romans 10:10)
❖ Repent of your sins, that is, turn your life
   around (Acts 17:30)
❖ Be baptized for the remission of sins. (Acts
   2:38)

NOTE:
*If you memorize these verses
and their location in the
Bible, you will be equipped
to show a friend how to be
saved.*

Other examples of easy-to-understand verses that
help you remain eligible for salvation include the
following:

❖ Grow in the grace and knowledge of Jesus.
   (I Peter 2:2; II Peter 3:18)
❖ Confess your faults one to another and pray
   one for another that you may be healed.
   (James 5:16)
❖ Do good to all men as you have opportunity.
   (Galatians 6:10)
❖ Live faithfully (obey Jesus) until death and
   receive a crown of life. (Revelations 2:10)

And there are many more easy-to-acquire diamonds
sparkling on the pages of the Bible. But now let's turn our
attention to some hard-to-discover gems that require
preparation and study.

PREPARING FOR BIBLE STUDY

To be prepared for Bible study, a person must prepare his heart and mind, decide on an appropriate time, move to a trouble-free area, and make certain that all needed books and supplies are readily available.

Preparing Our Hearts & Minds for Bible Study
To prepare our hearts and minds for Bible study, we should pray that the Lord will grant us wisdom to understand what we are reading—not necessarily all that we read but all that would be helpful at our present level of development. We should ask God to help us understand only what we are equipped to use and obey. No spiritual indigestion for us! Such a request I believe shows the proper humility toward God and toward Bible study. (James 1:22-25)

Deciding an Appropriate Time for Bible Study
When is an appropriate time for Bible study? It is a time when your mind is not overly tired and when you will not face interruptions. When would such a time be? Well, the evenings do NOT seem too favorable. At that time, you have friends who call you on the telephone or pop in for short visits. You, of course, are glad to see them, but they do cause an interruption. And besides, in the evenings your mind may already be tired from a long day's work or study. In my case, then, I have ruled out evening as a time for Bible study. Now, since you are at school or work during the day, what time is left for study? During your lunch hour, yes! But I believe there is a better time: During the early morning hours before the rest of the family arises. *And to get up that early would certainly require a great deal of love for the Lord, wouldn't it?* During these early morning hours, your mind would be fresh, and you certainly would not be interrupted by friend's calls or visit

or by the conversation by members of your own family. This is especially true if you have chosen a suitable area for Bible study.

Moving to a Trouble-Free Area for Bible Study

What is a trouble-free area for Bible study? The answer, of course, depends upon your particular home and the habits of your family. If you arise very early, you probably could study almost anywhere. *In my case, I prefer a kitchen table where the lighting is good and where there is plenty of room to lay out reference books.* But if your family normally has breakfast before your study time has passed, you will have to find a better location. So use your own judgment, but whatever place you choose, make certain there is a place to set the needed books and supplies.

Make Certain That Needed Books and Supplies Are Available

What books or supplies will you need for your study of the Bible? It depends on what you intend to accomplish during that study: learn for yourself alone or learn to teach other people. Regardless of your purpose, however, you will, of course, need a <u>Bible</u>, not just a <u>Bible</u> but more than one version of the <u>Bible.</u> And if you intend to teach, you may also need several types of reference books. And don't forget pens, pencils, paper, and other needed office supplies. A little bit of experience will show you what must be on hand to prevent interruptions in your study. These are useful hints on how to prepare for <u>Bible</u> study. We also have tips to remember while you are studying the Bible.

TIPS FOR STUDYING THE BIBLE

Below is an accurate quotation of parts of three verses of the Bible. Do they or do they not give the wrong impression when they are served together on the same plate?

- ❖ Judas went out and hanged himself. (Matthew 27:5)
- ❖ Go thou and do likewise. (Luke 10:37)
- ❖ What thou doeth, do quickly. (John 13:27)

Why are such "servings" of scripture misleading? They are misleading because they have been "taken out of context." To keep from taking verses "out of context" (or out of the situation in which they occur), we must consider:

- ❖ Who said the verse.
- ❖ To whom the verse was said.
- ❖ Why the verse was said.
- ❖ When the verse was said.
- ❖ The possible change in the meaning of the words used.

Remember Who Said or Did It

"You shalt not surely die!" Wow! That statement is in the Bible, so God must have decided to cancel death! No such luck! The Devil said it in Genesis 3:4, but he is the father of liars and a deceiver from the beginning. So don't depend on living forever—at least here on earth.

Remember to Whom It Was Said

In James 5:16 we read: Confess your faults one to another and pray one for another, that you may be healed." Well! That's all a person had to do: confess sins and have someone pray for him and he will be saved. So we don't need faith, confession, repentance or baptism, do we? Now, you KNOW THAT IS WRONG, don't you? Of course you do! The book of James was written to CHRISTIANS, who had already believed, confessed, repented and been baptized. And it was only after the sinner had obeyed God's commands and thus had been washed clean in the blood of Christ that James 5:16

applies—to Christians ONLY. So you see, it is important that you remember <u>to whom</u> a verse of scripture is addressed.

Remember Why It Was Said

In Galatians 6:5, the apostle Paul tells us that "every man shall bear his own burden." Wait a minute! I thought that Christians were taught to weep with those who weep (Romans 12:15); and in Galatians 6:2, we are told to bear one another's burdens. Which is it now—should we or should we not bear one another's burdens. Yes and No! If an erring brother is bowed with grief, yes, we should help bear his burden; and, yes, we should help bear the burden of grief when someone has lost a loved one or is otherwise greatly saddened. We should then sympathize. But no! If a brother refuses to <u>work</u> we should not help to bear any of his <u>financial burdens</u>. So you see the reason why a verse was written is important when we are trying to learn the meaning of a verse of scripture.

Also important to our use of a verse is to remember when that verse was written.

Remember When It Was Written

When was the last time that you brought a bull to church, to be used as a burned offering, as directed in Leviticus 1:2? This command does not apply to Christians who are not under the Law of Moses but are under the Perfect Law of Liberty. We must remember not to apply Old Testament commands to Christians who now live under the commands of the New Testament. And we must remember that in either the Old or the New Testaments the words may have changed meaning with the passage of many years.

Remember That Words Sometimes Change In Meaning

Luckily, not too many words have changed drastically in meaning with the passing of many years. But to really understand some scriptures, we must research to find the original meaning of some of them. For example, the word "hate" has changed in meaning. To explain: In the King James' Version of Luke 14:26, we find that a person must <u>hate</u> his father and mother to be Christ's disciple; and in Luke 18:20, Jesus tells us to <u>honor</u> our father and mother. Is this a conflict? No! At the time the New Testament was being written, the word "hate" meant "to love less." What, then, is being taught here? That we should honor our parents, but should love them less than we love the Lord Jesus.

For example, I know a young lady who was threatened with disinheritance by her family if she became a Christian. She did and they did; but she proved that she loved the Lord more than she loved her family. If you were faced with this situation would you show the same kind of courage? I pray that you will never be faced with such a decision, but that you would make a similar decision if required to do so, in spite of your love for your family.

And speaking of love, let's take a look at I Corinthians 13:3, as given in the King James Version of the Bible. There we see that "if we give all our possessions to feed the poor and have not <u>charity,</u> we are nothing. But doesn't "charity" mean to feed the poor? It does now, but it did not mean that when first written. At that time, charity meant "love." The verse then means that to help the poor without doing it through love is not profitable spiritually.

Let's also take another example of a word that good give a person some difficulty the word "strait." Notice that it is <u>not</u> spelled "straight" (meaning not crooked); but that being spelled "strait" means narrow and difficult. Such a meaning for "strait" is found in several Bible verses, among which is Matthew 7: 13, 14.

And there are many more words that have changed in the meaning during the passing of many years. To learn more about these words that have changed in meaning you should study a book which we recommended later in this chapter.

Before leaving our tips on Bible study, let's point out one more important fact: we remember best what we use.

Practice Improves Memory

One principle of learning is that we learn to do by doing. In the book of James, we also find that we learn to remember by doing. James points out that a person who reads the Bible without intending to obey it deceives his own self and will soon forget what he has read (James 1: 22-25). Such a haphazard use of the Bible would be a shameful use of the engrafted word which is able to save our souls (James 1:21). For us to grow and be blessed from Bible study, we must read it with the full intention of obeying what we learn.

But there are some parts of the Bible that we as Christians are not required to obey, even though we should study them.

PARTS OF THE BIBLE TO STUDY

What parts of the Bible should we study? To put it simply: all of it! But depending upon the circumstances, some parts of the Bible may be temporarily more appropriate than other parts. For example, if you wish to tell a friend how to be saved, you would not use passages from the Old Testament. After all, bullock burning is out of style and would be frowned upon by the Environmental

Protection Agency. Instead, you would use verses from the New Testament in teaching your friend how to be saved.

For another example: Suppose you wish to find information related to prophesies about the birth, death and resurrection of Christ. You would not go to the New Testament, because the prophecies about Christ were written long before his birth. Instead, you would find such prophecies in the Old Testament.

As stated before, you would not go to the Old Testament to find God's commands that apply to us today. You would, instead, go to the New Testament. Why, then, should we bother to study the Old Testament? Here are two good reasons for doing so:

❖ The Old Testament shows how God dealt with both sin and obedience and can serve as either a warnings or consolations. (I Corinthians 10: 1-11)

❖ The Old Testament is a schoolmaster to bring us to Christ (Galatians 3:24).

Why was the Old Testament a schoolmaster to bring us to Christ? Let's begin our answer to this question by referring to Matthew 5:17 in which Christ stated that he came to fulfill the law and the prophets. If he did not do so, he was a failure and could not be the Son of God as he claimed. But if Christ did fulfill all the law and the prophets completely, then He was indeed the Son of God. How can a person tell whether or not Christ fulfilled all these demands? By reading the law and the prophecies of the Old Testament and then checking out the New Testament to see if Christ actually did fulfill all the laws and all the prophecies. And He most certainly did!

But to understand the scriptures having prophecies about Christ, we often must make use of several types of study aids. What are these resources?

RESOURCES FOR UNDERSTANDING THE BIBLE

There are various types of resources to aid us in Bible study. Some are designed to help a beginner learn for his own benefit. Other, more advanced ones are needed by a person who is preparing to teach a Bible class. Let's briefly discuss these study aids, beginning with those for solely personal use.

Resources for Beginners
Resources for a beginning student of the Bible include Parallel Bibles, Study Bibles, and Bible Dictionaries. Let's briefly discuss the contents and use of each.

Parallel Bibles
Probably one of the most valuable aids for the beginning Bible study is a Parallel Bible, that is, a book that lines up several versions of the Bible side-by-side so that we can easily compare the wording of various versions. Such an arrangement actually serves as a simple commentary. Very helpful!

The Parallel Bible that I use is published by Zondervan and has four different versions of the Bible: King James, Amplified, New International, and New American Standard. These four Bible versions serve, to some degree, as both a limited dictionary and a limited commentary. For example, looking at Matthew 7:13 again, we find that the King James Version of the Bible describes the gate as "strait," while the Amplified, New International and New American Standard Versions use the word "narrow." In other instances, each of the four versions may differ in wording from the other three; and the different wording may help us to more readily grasp the intended meaning of a verse. The Parallel Bible is certainly very useful in our study. Here we have called attention to Zondervan's Parallel Bible. There are, however, many other good Parallel Bibles printed by other publishers, as is also true of publishers of Study Bibles.

Study Bible

Another valuable aid for Bible study is a Study Bible. In addition To being a complete Bible, this type of book contains the following:

- ❖ A guide for pronouncing proper names.
- ❖ Marginal references showing other related verses.
- ❖ References to varieties of wording in other Bible versions.
- ❖ Footnotes to explain some troublesome points.
- ❖ An index and limited concordance. (More about concordances later in this chapter)
- ❖ A limited atlas showing maps of Bible lands.

Because of the features named above, you could also classify a study Bible as a very limited commentary.

Another type study aid that helps us learn the meaning of Bible words is the Bible Dictionary.

Bible Dictionary

Where was Edom and who were the Edomites? A Bible Dictionary will answer such questions as this one as well as the following:

- ❖ How long was a cubit?
- ❖ How heavy was a talent?
- ❖ What is a carbuncle?
- ❖ How many mites make a farthing?
- ❖ How was wine made?
- ❖ What is a wineskin?

Learning answers to such questions as those help make some Bible verse more meaningful for both the learner and the teacher.

A new Christian, who is just beginning to study the Bible seriously, will certainly be helped in his efforts by Parallel Bibles, Study Bibles, and Bible Dictionaries. But at times, even with our best efforts the meaning of a verse of scripture may still be cloudy to us. At such times, we have another aid available to us, Christians more mature in the faith.

Christians More Mature in the Faith

Don't forget the help available from preachers, elders, deacons, and other Christians mature in the faith. To ask their help in Bible study is a compliment to these individuals. As you grow in the faith, other new Christians may soon be asking your help in Bible study. And before long you might be asked to teach the Bible class. In that case you, as a teacher will need additional study aids.

Resources for Bible Class Teachers

As a Bible class teacher, you would, of course, need all of the Bible study aids the already discussed; but, in addition, you might need concordances, commentaries, Topical Bibles, and books related to Christian living.

Concordance for Bible Teachers

Sometimes a person may know the words of a verse in the Bible but not know its location: book, chapter, and verse. If so, that's when a concordance comes in handy. In a concordance each word serves as the heading of a section that lists all the times that word occurs in the Bible. For example: The section headed "ABASE" lists three occurrences: Job 40:11, Ezekiel 21:26, and Daniel 4:37; and since the headings in the concordance are arranged in alphabetical order, the next section has the heading "ABASED," Matthew 13:12, Luke 14:11, Luke 18:24, and Philippians 4:12.

This is by no means a complete explanation on how to use a concordance; it is merely to let you know what a concordance is. More complete instructions for its use are given in the introductory material of the Concordance itself.

But sometimes a person cannot find all the information he needs by using all the references listed under a word in a Concordance. In this instance, a Topical Bible may be quite helpful.

Topical Bibles

Let's say to want to make a talk on the subject of "lending," as practiced in Old Testament days. *Why you ever would, I don't know. But this will serve as an example.* In a Concordance, you will find that there are eighteen verses that contain the word "lending"; but after looking them over carefully you still have not found all the information that you need for your talk. By going to the subject of "lending" in a Topical Bible you will also find other verses relating to "lending" that using the words "usury," "releases," "borrowing," "pledges," and "borrower." And for convenience these verses are not only referenced but are also given word for word, in one section of the Topical Bible. That would save you a great deal of flipping back and forth in your Bible to find them, wouldn't it?

Another type book that provides valuable information to a Bible class teacher is an expository dictionary of Bible words.

Expository Dictionaries

One such dictionary is Vines' Expository Dictionary of Old and New Testament Words. In this book, the English word is given; the various Greek words are then given to show the possible meanings of the English word; and scripture references for each possible meaning are listed.

For example, the English word "find" it has at least four different meanings in Greek. These meanings and a reference for each are as follows:

- ❖ To find with or without the previous search (Matthew 27:32).
- ❖ To find after a diligent search (Luke 2:16).
- ❖ To take or accept (Romans 7:21).
- ❖ To understand (Act's 25:25).

What we have said is not a complete explanation of the contents and the use of an expository dictionary of Bible words but enough has been given to let you know in general what an expository dictionary contains.

So, far, we have discussed books you might use in completing research for a Bible lesson. Now let's consider a type of book in which much of the research has been done for you: A book on Christian living.

Books on Christian Living

First, a word of caution: we should use the resource of Christian books with great care. Before using the material in any book written by mortal man, a teacher is responsible for checking the material for scriptural correctness. If the material is correct, it offers several advantages to the Bible class teacher. First, the books author may have saved you a great deal of work in research and in organizing material. And second, to read other people writing may stimulate your thinking and improve your lesson.

So much for our discussion of your new relationship with the Bible. Included were the topics of how the Bible serves you, how to prepare for Bible study, how to prevent using a verse "out of context," what parts of the Bible to study, and the resources for understanding the Bible. Hopefully, we have given you a good idea as to how you can prepare for your growth in Bible knowledge. And grow; I pray you will.

Now, let's go to Section 2 of this chapter to see what you have learned.

Section II: Let's See What You've Learned

1. For what reasons should a Christian learn all the commandments of God? _____

_____

_____

2. How can a Christian become a "conversational hog" where God is concerned? _____

_____

_____

3. How can you earn God's rating of noble?

_____

_____ and

_____

_____

4. Why can we say that the Bible serves you and me as a mirror? _____

_____

_____

5. What are the characteristics of the wisdom from above?

_____

_____

_____

6. Who alone possessed to the fullest all of the characteristics listed in your answer to 5 (above)

_____

7. Explain why a lack of purity in our lives could result in our death. _____

_____

_____

8. In what four ways does the Bible motivate us?

_____ ,

_____ ,

_____ , and

_____

9. In what ways can the Bible be compared to a diamond mine? _____

_____

_____

10. In what four ways should we prepare for Bible study?

_____ ,

_____ ,

_____ , and

_____

11. Since the Bible states that sins should be sent into the wilderness on a goat, this is how Christian and non-Christians should be forgiven. What is wrong with the conclusion drawn from this scripture? It is taken out of _____ because it does not

(1) _____
_____ and

(2) _____
_____

12. Since Christians are commanded to hate their parents, we should have nothing to do with them. Explain why this statement is wrong. _____
_____
_____

13. For what two reasons should we study the Old Testament? _____ _____ and
_____

14. How can you tell whether or not Christ fulfilled the law and the prophets? _____
_____
_____

15. What four resources are available to help a beginner study the Bible? _____,
_____,

_____, and

_____

16. What is meant by a "Parallel Bible"?_____

_____

_____

_____

17. Why can a Study Bible be rightly called a <u>limited</u> commentary? _____

_____

18. What use can be made of a Concordance?

_____

_____

_____

19. Why can we say that a Topical Bible is a good supplement to a Concordance? _____

_____

_____

_____

_____

Section III: Now Let's Get Personal

1. What use do you make of your "free" money? To answer this place a plus (+) before the two items you give the most money to; place a circle around the two which have second priority; and a minus (-) around the third priority. *Be honest now!*

    a. Church contribution.
    b. Buying cokes or candy.
    c. Helping a needy family.
    d. Building a religious library.
    e. Buying cigarettes.
    f. Paying to watch PG-13 movies.

2. Carefully examine your honest ratings, and tell what you believe that Jesus would think of your use of "free" money. _____

    _____

3. In the six spaces below, write in order what you believe Christians "free" money should be used for. (#1 = first choice, #2 = second choice, etc.)

1._____

_____

2._____

_____

3._____

_____

4._____

_____

5._____

_____

6._____

_____

4. A Christian's use of "free" money usually reveals how much he loves the Lord. Do you believe, or fail to believe, this is true? Please explain. _____

    _____

    _____

    _____

    _____

5. Has the Bible been a magnet, as it should be, to draw you to Christ? _____ _____.
    How can you increase its drawing effect on your life?

    _____

    _____

6. In serving as a mirror, what has the Bible revealed to you about your thoughts, words, and action?

    _____

    _____

    _____

    _____

7. How would you rate yourself on the wisdom that comes from above? Use "1" for Excellent; "2" for Good; "3" for Average; "4" for Poor; and "5" for Terrible. How do you think you can improve on each?

    _____Pure

    _____Peaceable

_____Gentle

_____Easy to be entreated

_____Merciful

_____Impartial

_____Without hypocrisy

8. Which of these characteristics, if any, do you need to improve on? _____

    _____

    _____ And how would you make such improvements? _____

    _____

    _____

9. In what way does the Bible most strongly motivate you to obey God? _____

    _____ Do you think your answer to this question will change as you become a stronger Christian? _____

10. When is the best time for you personally to study the Bible? _____

    _____ Why do you say so? _____

    _____

    _____

11. What aids do you now possess to help you study the Bible? _____

_____

_____

12. What additional study aids, if any, do you plan to add to your religious library? _____

_____

_____

13. Do you plan someday to become a Bible teacher? _____ _____ If so, what

preparation should you NOW be making? _____

_____

_____

14. If you do not feel that you can ever teach, what other tasks will you be able to do in the Lord's work?

_____

_____

_____

15. If you answer question 14, volunteer to help the church by doing any related tasks available. *A Christian life is one of service – service to God and service to our fellow man.*

Chapter V. YOUR NEW RELATIONSHIP WITH CHURCH LEADERS

Section 1: Let's Talk About It.

Onward, ever onward sped the thundering hoof beats as the sheriff's posse relentlessly pursued the horse thief. At last he was captured. Justice then was swift and certain; and soon the thief was swing and kicking in a wild effort to remove the rope from his neck, but to no avail. The authority which the horse thief had rejected had decreed this horrible punishment.

In more modern times, when the authority of the law has been rejected, the criminal may not suffer the sentence of death; but may, instead, be separated from society. Thus, prisons are built to protect society from the misdeeds of the criminal.

Now, in my own mind's eye, I go back to my childhood; and I well remember that I was neither hung from a sycamore tree nor imprisoned when I rejected the authority of my father and mother. However, if memory serves me well, I did feel like I was receiving capital punishment from the razor strap, and it did seem that I was serving a life sentence as I was forced to stand in a corner while the other children were outside playing. But looking back from the vantage point of grown-up life, I now see that my parents actually were showing a great deal of patience in my discipline.

A great deal more patience, however, is shown today by the Good Lord if we reject His authority. He is long suffering toward us, hoping that none of us will suffer the eternal death of Hell (II Peter 3:9). But our punishment, though possibly not so severe, is nevertheless certain. Perhaps, if our conscience is tender, we will feel the aching pain of guilt. If so, be thankful: the Lord is treating us as His sons, hoping that we will soon repent of our misdeeds (Hebrew 12:5-7). Or perhaps, working through other people, the Lord will allow us to be chastised. In either case, God is showing us His "tough love" in an effort to provoke us to love and good works (Hebrew 10:24). So, we should be thankful for the punishment. We should kiss the whip that scourges us, so to speak, as pointed out in the poem "Kiss the Whip" located on page A-3, in the back of the book. Yes, we should thank God for chastisement that lead us to repentance, that rescues our souls from the Devil, and that returns us to "favored-child" status with the Good Lord.

So far, we have talked about the possible punishment that may come if we reject authority. Now, let's consider the types of authorities that exercise control over us. There are two general types: governmental and religious. Governmental authorities include city, county, state and federal government. *We discuss our relationship of governmental authorities in Chapter IX of this book.* And religious authority begins with God.

God's authority is supreme. He is in command, along with those to whom He has delegated some or all of His authority. God has delegated SOME of His authority to civil government (Romans 13:1,2). But God has delegated ALL of His authority to Jesus Christ (Matthew 28:18). Jesus, in turn, has delegated SOME, but not ALL, of His authority for church leadership to elders, the overseers of the church.

In this chapter we discuss the limited authority of elders, their qualifications, their duties, and our relationship to them.

THE LIMITED AUTHORITY OF ELDERS

Why are elders' authority said to be "limited"? Because Christ refused to delegate one type of authority to them but did fully delegate to them another type of

authority. What type of authority is forbidden to elders?
Authority to change the meaning of God's Word. For
example, let's consider the mission of the church. Briefly
stated, the church is commanded "Go into all of the world
and teach all nations...to observe all things which I have
commanded you." (Matthew 28:19,20). Can an eldership
then scripturally decide: "Forget about the gospel; we will
stress basketball and bowling. That will draw more people
to Church. No! An eldership does not have the authority
to change any of Christ's commands or teachings.

Then what authority has Christ delegated to elders?
The answer is: the right to lead in matters of expediency
that is to work out the details on how to carry out Christ's
commands. For example, we Christians are to meet on the
first day of the week—but at what hours? The elders are
free to decide this. The elders are also free to decide
whether we stand during service or if we are provided with
pews; and if so, what type of pews.

For another example, the Bible commands the
church to "go teach." How should we go: walking, on
horseback, in a car, in an airplane, or in a boat? The elders
are free to make this type of decision. And how should we
teach: in classes, in an auditorium, on the radio, or on TV.
The elders can decide on all of these matters of expediency.
But they do not have authority to change the gospel, and
they would be condemned by God if they did try to do so
(Galatians 1:8,9).

So you see, an elder must have good judgment; and
before making a decision, he must first decide whether it is
a matter of scriptural correctness or of expediency. And his
other demanding duties complied with his limited authority
demand that an elder be well qualified for his office. This
being so, let's first discuss the qualification for an elder.

QUALIFICATION OF ELDERS

Since you may be a new or recent convert to Christianity why should we here and now discuss the qualifications of a church leader? There are two basic reasons. First, if we look at the qualifications of an elder spelled out in I Timothy, Chapter 3, and in Titus, Chapter 1, we will come to this conclusion: With six notable exceptions, all of the qualifications of an elder are also those which <u>any</u> Christian should possess.

And second, the goal of every male Christian should be to qualify himself as an elder. Why? Because it is an office of great service. It does have its concerns and heartaches. But by working faithfully in his offices, an elder may be helpful in seeing that many beloved members stay on the road to heaven. It is an office of WORK, one that demands that an elder lay down his <u>living</u> for other church members. Yes! It is a work but it is also an office of honor, highly to be desired. And with that, we spell out the second reason for acquainting you now with an elder's qualification: To give you time to set development goals so that you can qualify for serving as an elder.

List of an elder's qualifications, along with a brief discussion of each, follows. In the first list, we enumerate elder's qualifications that should be common to all Christians.

Elder Qualifications Common To All Christians

Remember that the following qualifications for an elder should also be possessed by any Christian. So you might use them as a checklist.

❖ <u>Blameless:</u> Cannot be honestly accused of misbehavior. *Many of the following qualifications if violated would also violate the qualification of blameless.*

- ❖ <u>Good Behavior:</u>   Following all of God's rules for words and action.
- ❖ <u>Not given to wine:</u> Drunkenness can cause all kinds of misbehavior, sets a bad example for other church members, and brings reproach upon the church.
- ❖ <u>No striker:</u> Not highly argumentative and not apt to abuse a person physically.
- ❖ <u>Not self-willed:</u>   Not determined to have one's own way regardless of the cost.
- ❖ <u>Not soon angered:</u> With the rise of anger, judgment declines and trouble often starts.
- ❖ <u>Not a brawler:</u>   When anger rises, the possibility of shouting and fighting can erupt. Such action brings dishonor on both the individual and the church.
- ❖ <u>Holy:</u>   Set apart from worldly words and action. Living to please Jesus.
- ❖ <u>Temperate:</u> Not given to excessive use of any substance, including food. (ouch!)
- ❖ <u>Sober:</u> Using good judgment in an earnest effort to lead a Christian life.
- ❖ <u>Vigilant:</u> Being ever watchful so the devil will not sneak up on our blind side (I Peter 5:8).
- ❖ <u>Patient:</u>   Keep on keeping on in our Christian endeavors in spite of obstacles and setbacks.
- ❖ <u>Not greedy for money:</u> Being satisfied with what the Lord has given us. The love of money is the root of all evil (I Timothy 6:10).
- ❖ <u>Not covetous:</u> Does not grumble about that which God has <u>not</u> given. Is not willing to disobey God to obtain what God has not given (Hebrews 13:5).

❖ <u>Holding fast the Word of God:</u> Not willing to vary from God's revealed will. This requires regular Bible study. Daily study is highly recommended.

❖ <u>Given to hospitality:</u> Many sales are made by a salesman sharing a meal with a prospective customer. Christians can also make use of meals to develop friendships and even lead others to Christ.

So far, we have discussed the qualifications of elders that are common to all Christians. Now, let's turn our attention to the other qualification required of elders.

Other Qualifications Required of Elders

Included in the other qualifications required of elders are not being a novice, desiring the office of an elder, the husband of one wife, ruling his house well, having the ability to exhort the brethren, and having the ability to convince the gainsayers.

Not a novice

(a new or recent convert): Such a person would not have a good enough command of the scriptures to serve as an elder. Neither would he have had enough time to "weed out" some possible troublesome habits and attitudes. Furthermore, the scripture warns that a novice could easily be lifted up with pride and thus fall into the condemnation of the devil (I Timothy 3:6.)

Must desire the office

No one should be forced against his will to be an elder. Such person would probably lack the dedication required to be a successful elder.

The husband of one wife

This requirement rules out unmarried men and men with more than one wife (polygamy). (With more than one wife, a man might be too busy refereeing to be available to perform an elder's duties.) Also ruled out are those men who have remarried after a <u>non-scriptural</u> divorce. Such men would be setting a poor example for the congregation.

Rules His Own Home Well

A person who cannot lead his house *with few members* cannot hope to lead the Church *with many members.*

Able to Exhort the Brethren

As a watchman for the souls of church members, an elder may see evidence of sins, other weaknesses, and failures to engage in work for the Lord. In any of these instances, the elder should attempt to exhort the members to love and good works by speaking the truth in a loving way.

Convincing the Gainsayers

In some instance, a church member may truthfully and strongly believe some ideas that are in error. In other instances, those not in church may honestly believe errors and may strongly defend their point of view. Because of his depth of Bible knowledge, an elder should be able to convince those inside or outside the Church of the true Bible meaning of related scriptures. This is but one of the many duties which an elder performs.

DUTIES OF AN ELDER

In discussing the qualifications of an elder, we did by necessity include, by direct statement or implication, some of the elders' duties. Included in these were the following:

- Living an example for the church (I Peter 5:3).
- Being constantly vigil in keeping members faithful.
- Being a devoted student of the Bible.
- Exhibiting hospitality.
- Ruling his house well; keeping his children submissive.
- Exhorting Christians who are not living a dedicated Christian life.
- Correcting scriptural errors.

Perhaps one of the duties listed above might require more complete discussion: The one concerning an elder being an example for the Church. To live such an example, an elder should:

- Set an example of regular church attendance.
- Visit the sick, shut-ins, and those in prison.
- Visit and comfort families saddened by death.
- Regularly attend all elders' meetings.
- Contribute to discussions in elders' meetings.
- Publicly support decisions reached by elders collectively even if he opposed that decision during the elder's meeting. *Unless, of course, that decision is unscriptural.*
- Visiting and exhorting members who seem to be drifting away.
- Helping to select other elders and deacons.

You can see then that an elder will be a very busy man and that his duties are plentiful. He must not act as a dictator (I Peter 5:2, 3), but must instead lead by example and by loving exhortation. We should honor and appreciate our hard-working and dedicated elders. And that is one of the relationships we should have with our elders: appreciation of their good work.

RELATIONSHIP OF ELDERS AND MEMBERS

We should honor and respect elders because they watch for our souls. And we should understand that they are carrying a heavy burden on their backs. This being so, we should never expect an elder—or anyone else—to be perfect. We should understand that as human beings they have weaknesses just as we do; but that they are always trying to grow closer to the Lord Jesus and are encouraging us to do so.

What should we do when we think an elder has sinned? We should at first talk to him *in private* and otherwise follow the instructions given in Matthew 18:15-17. *NEVER GOSSIP.*

What should we do when you think that the eldership has made a wrong decision in a matter of expediency? Go talk to an elder *or the leadership as a whole.* If he refuses to change, drop the subject. *NEVER GOSSIP.* He may refuse to change because he may know other facts which you don't know—facts he is not at liberty to make public.

But now, let's flip over the coin and look at the other side. What if the problem is one of your own and not one of the elders? For example, let's say that someone has informed the elders that you have sinned. *If they haven't talked to you about it, they have been guilty of the sin of gossip and violating Matthew 18:15-17.* But let's say the elder approaches you in hopes of exhorting and encouraging you to repent. If you are not guilty of the sin reported, how would you react? Rear up on your hind legs and spit fire? No! The elder is watching for your soul (Hebrews 13:17); and that would be poor thanks for his trying to help you, wouldn't it? Instead of exploding you should patiently inform the elder of the truth (Ephesians 4:15).

But suppose the elder has been correctly informed of your sin, and that he approaches to exhort and encourage you. How should you react? Humbly accept the correction, repent, ask the elder to pray for you, and thank him for his loving concern for your soul. Now let's look at another type of trouble you might experience: a serious illness or death in your family. Can an elder help you? Yes! His visits and prayers can be most comforting. Elders are great in love and sympathy. Don't overlook this source of comfort.

By now, you should have a good general idea of the limitation of elder authority, the qualification and duties of elders, and our relationship to them. Have you learned a great deal? We'll find out when you work the next section of the chapter, titled "Let's See What You've Learned." In that section, we also present a few additional facts to further acquaint you with the job of elders.

Section II: Let's See What You've Learned

THE AUTHORITY OF CHRIST

1. After Christ arose from the dead, he was given _____ authority both in _____ and on _____ (Matthew 28:18).

2. How much authority does Christ, therefore, have in spiritual matters? _____

3. After Christ went to heaven, how did He continue to teach (remind) His disciples?_____

(John 14: 25,26)

4. Lead by the _____, the disciples wrote the books of the New Testament, which are teachings and reminders directly from _____ and therefore carry his full authority.

5. Authorized Christian doctrine (teaching) is therefore found in _____ _____ (II Timothy 3:16).

6. In the New Testament, the teaching of Christ is referred to as the Word of God, the truth, the gospel, or the faith. After the faith was delivered to the saints, was it then subject to addition, subtraction, or change? (Jude 3)

7. Anyone who perverts (changes) the gospel is _____ (Galatians 1:6-9).

8. In the following list, circle the ones who have been authorized by Christ to change the spiritual doctrines of the New Testament. (Galatians 1:6-9)*Elders *Preachers *Deacons *Angels *Neither angels nor men

9. What did Paul say would take place after his departure?

_____

_____

_____ _____And what group of people would be responsible? _____

_____

(Acts 20:29,30)

10. How can we tell whether an elder, preacher, or teacher is attempting to change the gospel?

    a. _____

       (I John 4:1)

    b. _____

       (Acts 17:11)

11. If an elder, preacher or teacher attempts to change the gospel, should we accept the change?

_____

    a. _____

       (Acts 4:19)

    b. _____

       (Romans 3:4)

THE AUTHORITY OF ELDERS

1. Elders are told to _____ (I Peter 5:12).

2. Elders are _____ who watch over our souls (Hebrews 13:17).

3. Elders decide on matters of expediency—how best to carry out Christ's commands.

112

"Listed on page 113 are several commands of Christ, with a space provided where you should list the decisions an eldership might make to carry out these commands." (None of these decisions must conflict with instructions given by Christ.)

CHRIST' COMMAND   NATURE OF ELDER'S DECISION

Go Teach (Matthew 28:19,20)

_____   _____

Go Baptize (Matthew 28:19,20)

_____   _____

Assemble Christians (Hebrews 10:25)

_____   _____

On First Day of Week (Acts 20:7)

_____   _____

THE DUTIES OF ELDERS

1. Tend _____

    Not for _____

    Not as _____

    But rather serving as _____

    for the flock (I Peter 5:1-3).

2. Manage his own _____ and the _____ (I Timothy 3:4, 5).

3. Give _____

    (Titus 1:9).

4. Refute _____
   (Titus 1:9).

5. Visit the _____
   (James 5:14).

6. Watch

   _____

   _____ _____

   (Hebrews 13:17).

7. In addition to the duties already specified, an elder performs the duties required of all other church members.

THE RELATIONSHIP BETWEEN ELDERS AND DEACONS

1. The word "deacon" was derived from, the Greek word "diakonos", meaning "servant", which accurately describe a deacon's function. A deacon does <u>not</u> rule; but instead, working under the oversight of the elders, he <u>serves</u> the congregation.

2. Deacons were originally chosen to _____ (Acts 6:2-4), that is to accomplish the routine tasks which keep the church functioning smoothly. Included are such tasks as preparing rooms for meetings, distributing help to

the needy, and performing other tasks required for putting into action the decisions made by the elders on matters of expediency.

3. In addition to the tasks already stated, a deacon performs all duties required of other church members— all under the oversight of the elders.

THE RELATIONSHIP BETWEEN ELDERS AND PREACHERS

1. The Apostle Paul, in addressing the young preacher, Timothy, pointed out the two chief responsibilities on a preacher:

    a. Set the believers an example in _____

    _____

    (I Timothy 4:12) and

    b. Attend to _____, to

    _____

    _____ (I Timothy 4:13).

2. To emphasize the dedication to duty that a preacher should have, the apostle Paul also charges Timothy to

_____

_____

(II Timothy 4:1, 2).

3. Like a deacon, a preacher does not rule; but instead, working under the oversight of the elders, a preacher serves the congregation with spiritual food. In fact, to show his respect for the eldership, the preacher is told

_____

_____

(I Timothy 5:1).

4. Under the oversight of the elders, a preacher also performs all duties required of other church members.

THE RELATIONSHIP BETWEEN ELDERS AND OTHER CHURCH MEMBERS

1. Church members are told not to _____ an elder (I Timothy 5:1) but to count him worthy of _____ especially if he also labors in _____ and _____ (I Timothy 5:17).

2. Church members are told not to _____ _____ against an elder except on the evidence of _____ (I Timothy 5:19).

3. Church members are told to be _____ _____ to elders (I Peter 5:5) and to _____ (Hebrews 13:17).

4. Like the people of Berea, Christians also have the duty to receive _____ with all _____ and search

116

to see if the things taught are so (Acts 17:11).

5. After learning the truth about matters, Christians have the duty to walk _____ and to have _____ with one another (I John 1:7).

6. Christians are also told to keep _____ _____ in the _____ (Ephesians 4:3).

7. Christians are also told to do_____ _____ especially to those of _____ (Galatians 6:10).

<u>Section III: Now Let's Get Personal</u>

For each question, circle the letter before each correct answer(s).

1. If you are positive that a brother has sinned, to whom should you <u>first</u> report it?
    a. To the elders.
    b. To the preacher.
    c. To the deacons.
    d. To the sinner himself.
2. In your opinion, which of the following would be most patient with you if you sinned?
    a. Your mother and father.
    b. Your elders.
    c. The preacher.
    d. God.
3. For what reason should a male new convert learn about the qualifications for elder?

      a. Most of the qualifications also apply to every Christian.
      b. They help us train during the years to become elders.
      c. They act as a checklist to show us how to improve.
      d. They help us find fault with our eldership.

4. A new convert would not be appointed as an elder because:
      a. He does not have enough friends to vote him in.
      b. He would create jealousy among the other new converts.
      c. He has not mastered scripture well enough.
      d. He might be lifted up with pride.

5. The duties of an elder include:
      a. Regular attending church.
      b. Devoutly studying the Bible.
      c. Helping to select other elders.
      d. Exhorting members to go to work for the Lord.

6. If an elder approaches a member to exhort him to repent of a sin that the member has not committed, the member should:
      a. Tell the elder abruptly to get the facts before he talks.
      b. Tell him you are moving your membership.
      c. Tell him you will whip the person who falsely reported him.
      d. Thank the elder for his loving concern.

7. If an elder has sinned what should you do first?
      a. Tell him to shape up or ship out.
      b. Inform the congregation of this disgrace.
      c. Ask the elder about the incident.
      d. Move your membership to another congregation.

8. How you rate yourself on the qualifications for elders that are common to all Christians? On the space before each item place a "5" for excellent; a "4" for good; a "3" for average; a "2" for poor; and a "1" for terrible.

_____ Blameless

_____ Temperate

_____ Good Behavior

_____ Sober

_____ Not Given to Wine

_____ Vigilant

_____ Not Argumentative

_____ Patient

_____ Not self-willed

_____ Not greedy for money

_____ Not soon angered

_____ Not covetous

_____ Not a brawler

_____ Holding fast the Word of God

_____ Holy

_____ Given to hospitality

9. Take your three worst items and plan to start your improvement. Then work on the next worst three, etc.

10. How do you plan to make such improvements?

Chapter VI. YOUR NEW RELATIONSHIP WITH YOUR SPIRTUAL FAMILY

Section 1: Let's Talk About It.

Jesus said that those who left their family for his sake and for the sake of the gospel would receive back here a hundred fold and in the world to come eternal life. (Mark 10:29, 30). As is always true, Jesus knew what He was talking about: My family now numbers in the hundreds; and the relationship between me and my brothers and sisters in Christ grows deeper and deeper with each passing day, surpassing even the closeness between me and my physical family.

Yes! It's a close relationship between brothers and sisters in Christ; but the very closeness may sometimes cause problems if we fail to give that relationship what we really owe it. What do we really by owe that relationship? To put it in a nutshell, what we owe that relationship is to provoke one another to love and good works (Hebrews 10: 24). But to really fulfill the requirements of this verse in it's the entirety we must have the following:

- ❖ Fellowship.
- ❖ Communication.
- ❖ Understanding.
- ❖ Christian attitudes.
- ❖ Christian actions.
- ❖ Christian words.

In this chapter, we discuss each of these six requirements for reducing or eliminating friction between church members.

THE DEBT OF CHRISTIAN FELLOWSHIP OWED

During various stages of the creation of the world, our Heavenly Father examined his work and rates it "GOOD." There was, however, one condition that God declared was "NOT GOOD." He said it was not good that man should be alone; so God gave man the companionship of woman.

Throughout the ages, the principles held true: Man should not live alone but should enjoy the fellowship of other human beings, male or female. This principle is stated or clearly implied by many passages in the Bible, for example Hebrews 10:25 which states that we should not forsake the assembling of ourselves together.

Since fellowship is counted so important in the scriptures, we will discuss the following about it.

- ❖ The purpose of fellowship.
- ❖ Requirement for regular assembly with its church.
- ❖ Fellowship in the assembly of the Church.
- ❖ Fellowship in smaller groups.

The Purpose of Fellowship

The purpose of fellowship is to promote growth in love and to encourage, build up and strengthen one another. We are to comfort and edify one another (I Thessalonians 5:11); and we are to preserve those things which make for peace (Romans 14:19). We comfort one another with a sympathizing tear (Romans 12:15) when a brother or sister has suffered a great loss, for example a death in the family. And we should abandon things which cause friction such as envy, harsh words, and selfishness. These statements are equally true while we are in the assembly or away from it.

The Requirements for Regular Assembly With the Church

"Because evil will abound, the love of many shall wax cold" (Matthew 24:12). During the life of Christ, the evil world was not His friend, and many times, even the Son of God was grieved and was drawn to prayer because so much evil surrounded him. And the world today is also filled with evil and temptations, which plague us as Christians. We must be careful, however, not to drown ourselves in <u>fretting</u> about the evil because such fretting will lead us into sin (Psalms 37:8). Instead, we should first pray and then do whatever we can to correct the situation—but don't worry.

And in particular we should be careful not to envy the "fun" being "enjoyed" by sinners (Psalms 37:1); because such envy is the first step down the road to joining the evildoer. So, don't be envious; just remember that the wicked will soon be punished and that you don't wish to suffer with them.

With the sinful people of the world around us we tend to lose our zeal for the Lord and with it the desire to grow as a Christian. Spiritually speaking, our "go-machine" seems to "run out of gas." And just where is the station for refilling our empty tank? At church, in the assembly with our brothers and sisters in Christ, and with Christ in our midst.

Not only do we gain spiritual strength from attending church services, but we also prove our love for Christ by doing so. Why? Well, look at the following reasons:

❖ We show our love for Christ by attending his memorial service, observing the Lord's Supper (I Corinthians 11:26). *Would you miss a friend's funeral service?*

❖ We show that Jesus is our BEST friend because Jesus is in our midst at church when we gathered in His name (Matthew 18:20). *With whom else would you rather be?*

❖ We show we love Jesus by keeping his command to attend Church (Hebrews 10:25; John 14:15), by assembling on the first day of the week (Acts 20:7; I Corinthians 16:2), and by assembling at the time decided by the elders (Hebrews 13:17).

While at Church, there are several types of fellowship that we may enjoy.

Fellowship Enjoyed in the Assembly of the Church

Fellowship in the assembly consists of informal visitation and formal worship. And what can surpass the joy of informal visits with beloved brothers and sisters in Christ, before and after worship services. Only one thing can surpass it: The joy of blending our hearts together in worship of our loved and loving Heavenly Father. This we do in the acts of worship which include prayer, singing, study of the Bible, observing the Lord's Supper, and the giving of our means. Let's briefly discuss each of the acts of worship.

Prayer. Why do we pray? For a t least six reasons:
❖ To praise God (Matthew 6:9).
❖ To pray that his will be done on earth (Matthew 6:10).
❖ To ask for the necessities of life (Matthew 6:11).
❖ To ask forgiveness for sins (Matthew 6:12).
❖ To ask for strength to overcome sin (Matthew 6:13).
❖ To pray for a brother who has confessed sins (James 5:16).

Singing to God and to one Another As we lift our voices in song we serve a two-fold purpose: (1) To praise God (Ephesians 5:19) and (2) to teach and admonish one another (Colossians 3:16). It should be remembered about singing, however, that we should understand what we are singing (I Corinthians 14:15). Suppose, then, that you don't understand the words of a song? If so, on the first opportunity, learn what the words mean by asking a person who is more mature in the Lord.

Bible Study
Christians should be taught to observe all things which Christ has commanded (Matthew 28:20). Where will you find Christ's commands? Jesus speaks to us directly in the gospel books of Matthew, Mark, Luke, and John. And He speaks to us indirectly through the Holy Spirit in Acts, Revelation, and in the 21 letters of the New Testament: Romans through Jude (John 14:26; John 16:13). Will you have any trouble during Bible study at home in understanding the meanings of the 27 books of the Old Testament (not to mention the 39 books of the Old Testament)? If you are like me, you sometimes will.

In II Peter 3:16, the Apostle Peter pointed out two things concerning the writings of the Apostle Paul:

❖ They contain some things which are hard to understand.

❖ Some unlearned people twist the meanings of Paul's writings to their own destruction.

Say, that's two good reasons why we need to engage in Bible study <u>at church.</u> One, to clear up the meanings of hard-to-understand passages, and two, to prevent us from destroying ourselves spiritually by getting a twisted, incorrect meaning from scriptures.

Now, here's another benefit of Bible study at church: We gain the benefit of the research work done by the teacher of the group. To adequately prepare a lesson, a dedicated teacher will spend many hours of research, using books and other resources which may not be available to us. And in only about an hour of class, we gain the benefit of the teachers many hours of study. And that is highly efficient learning, my friend: One hour invested on your part to gain several hours worth of understanding.

Giving of our Means
In Psalms 89:11 the Psalmist said to Heavenly Father:
> "The heavens are thine; the earth is also thine, the world and all that is in it, thou hast founded them."

In one sense of the word, then, it is impossible to give anything material to the Lord because he, as the creator of the world, already owns everything. In what sense do we really give to the Lord? Let me answer with this illustration. Little Molly, who is five years old, said she was giving her father a new briefcase for Christmas. "How can you, a child, pay for such an expensive gift?" asked her neighbor. "My daddy will give me the money," replied Molly. What was the real gift she gave her father? The briefcase. No! The real gift was her love!

And essentially that's what our giving shows our Heavenly Father: That we love him. Why do I say that giving shows our love? Among other things, giving shows that we are obeying a command of God; and obedience is an acid test of love (John 14:15). Not only that but giving to the Lord helps our love grow, just as the love of a Mother grows more and more as she serves and sacrifices for a child.

Then, too giving helps to make the giver happy (Acts 20:35). Why? Because giving makes our love for God to grow; and the greatest happiness here on earth comes from loving others – God or other people.

How much should we give to the Lord? In answering this question, we first should ask, "How much of material goods has the Lord given to us?" Here, in the United States of America, we have been of all nations most blessed with material possessions. Having seen several nations in the Far East, I can tell you that the poorest people among us are rich compared with many people of the world. And remember this, "To whom much is given, much will be expected (Luke 12:48).

How much then should you give? You alone can answer this question; but to help you decide, the Bible gives several guidelines. Here they are:

❖ Give bountifully (II Corinthians 9:6). You will reap bountifully in either material for spiritual benefits whichever the Lord knows will be for your highest good.

❖ Give cheerfully (II Corinthians 9:7). Have you ever received a gift when the giver's attitude clearly showed that he really did not want to give it? How did you feel? A begrudging gift does not show love, but rather covetousness. I believe God feels slighted with such a gift.

❖ Give as You have Purposed in your heart. No one should dictate what you must give: 5%, 10%, 15%, etc. you must decide that for yourself. In my opinion, however, 10% percent is a good starting place before we begin to grow in the grace of giving (II Peter 3:18).

❖ Growing in the Grace of Giving. Perhaps one of the best examples of churches that had grown in the grace of giving were the churches of Macedonia. These churches were liberal in spite of their own poverty because they first gave themselves to the Lord (II Corinthians 8:1-5). And that pretty well helps to determine how much we give to the Lord, the degree to which we have given ourselves to the Lord, the degree to which we have denied ourselves, the degree to which we are willing to give sacrificially. As a Christian, more and more, we learn to deny ourselves; more and more, we learn to shoulder our own cross; and more and more we learn to follow close to Jesus.

❖ Give sacrificially. Sacrificial giving is easy to do if we remember two things. First, remember the great sacrifices the Lord Jesus made in leaving the perfection of heaven, living a tiring and persecuted life for our benefit, and then dying on a cruel cross. Would you or I begrudge a sacrificial gift for such a savior? And second, in a more selfish vein, let me point out that happiness does not consist of the things we own but rather of the things that don't own us. Happiness grows as we sacrifice more and more for the Lord. The happiness consists of the things we can do without!

That concludes our discussion of the fellowship that we Christians enjoy at church in a large group. However, we are also blessed with fellowship in small groups, sharing a meal in a café, or having fellowship in the home of one of the church member.

Fellowship Enjoyed in Small Groups

Sharing a meal by two or more families at a café is an ideal way to become better acquainted, to develop friendships and to help encourage and strengthen brothers and sisters in Christ. Then, too, as already pointed out, when we share a meal with a prospective Christian, it develops a bond that later may lead the prospect to accept Christ as his or her savior.

128

Sharing fellowship with several families in the home of a member can be more organized and perhaps more beneficial. Advanced preparations for such a fellowship might include making a list of questions which will not only "break the ice" but also provide background information on the members, thus helping them to become better acquainted with each other. Some examples of the type of questions that could be used are as follows:

- ❖ Where were you born?
- ❖ When were you born? (Ladies with more than one 39th birthday need not answer this question.)
- ❖ How did you meet your husband/wife?
- ❖ Where did you go to school?
- ❖ What do you remember most about the family you grew up in?
- ❖ What do you remember most about the school you attended?
- ❖ Who was your favorite teacher and why?
- ❖ Up to date, what has been the happiest/saddest moment of your life?
- ❖ What has been your most embarrassing moment?
- ❖ When and where were you baptized?
- ❖ What is your favorite color/cold drink/dessert/entrée?
- ❖ If you could live life over again, which event would you change?
- ❖ What is the greatest talent you can give to the Lord?
- ❖ What major sickness or accident have you suffered?

❖ In the house you grew up in, what kind of plumbing did it have?

These are but a few of the many questions that could be asked to create better understanding of our brothers and sisters. Notice in this exercise that communication is taking place between all those present.

THE DEBT OF CHRISTIAN COMMUNICATION WE OWE

If you will pardon the personal references, when I was about ten years old I suffered a boil on my right kneecap. It kept getting bigger, aching, and throbbing, getting bigger, aching, and throbbing until at last, in spite of my fear of the knife, I asked the doctor to lance it. With the lancing came a relief of pressure so great that I almost passed out from sheer relief. If I had not relieved the poisoning of the boil, my entire leg could have swelled and possibly I could have lost my right leg.

How does this illustration tie in with communication? Let's say that a brother has sinned against you and that you deeply resent what he has done. The resentment, if not relieved, lies there festering like a boil; and you just don't feel right toward that brother because of the ache and throb of injured pride. If you don't relieve that ache, what happens? It gets worse and worse, possibly leading to a deep-seated malice and the loss of your own soul.

What could prevent this loss? Communication! Go talk to your brother to "lance the boil" so that normal loving relations can be restored. What exact process should you use in the talk? The formula is found in Matthew 18:15-17 and includes:

❖ Go talk with your brother (YES! You are told to do this.)
❖ If your brother repents, forgive him.

❖ If he will not change, then take two or three witnesses and talk with him again.
❖ If he's still will not change, tell it to the Church.

If you do these things you have discharged your duty as a Christian.

But let me point out one precaution to observe before you go talk to an erring brother: When you first go to talk, ask questions, to insure that you have not been mistaken about the "sins." Don't start with an accusation. By doing so you may burn all bridges to reconciliation. And always remember to speak the truth in love.

But now, suppose the shoe is on the other foot; it is you who has sinned against a brother. What should you do—wait him to approach you? No! You are commanded to go to your brother and make things right as soon as possible (Matthew 5:23, 24).

But how important does God consider communication when a sin has been committed? So important that God commands each party to go to the other thus insuring that communication does take place. We are never supposed to fertilize injured pride with silent pouting. Instead, we must communicate.

Now suppose that no sin has taken place, how can we insure communication does proceed harmoniously? Here are some great tips:

❖ Be slow to speak and quick to hear (James 1:19).
❖ Never fall in love with the sound of your own voice. Don't talk too much (Proverbs 10:19).
❖ Speak the truth in a loving way (Ephesians 4:15).
❖ Keep your speech pure (Colossians 4:6).
❖ Don't brag on yourself (I Corinthians 1:31). In particular, don't brag about what you are

going to do tomorrow. But instead say, "If the Lord wills, I will do "so and so.""" (James 4:13-16).

❖ Never gossip (Proverbs 26:20). Any evil report, whether true or false, is gossip. Don't do it! It causes trouble.

❖ Give God the credit for your good deeds (Matthew 5:16). *Where did you get the life and strength to do those good deeds?*

While discussing Christian communication, we stressed the use of talking to avoid the creation of hard feelings and to relieve hard feelings if a sin has been committed. But communication is necessary, too, if Christian understanding of each person is to develop.

THE DEBT OF CHRISTIAN UNDERSTANDING WE OWE

Sometimes, when we witness the words or actions of a Christian brother, whether new or old in the faith, we ask ourselves, "How in the world can a person who is a Christian do such a thing?" This question may make us fret, make us feel ashamed of the brother, or tend to weaken our faith if we do not understand the warfare going on inside each Christian. This warfare is in you, in me, and in every child of God; and it will last as long as we are alive here on Earth.

Three facts will help us understand this warfare and why our brother sometimes acts the way they do:

❖ Most Christians wish to do right but are weak.

❖ A few brethren will be hypocrites.

❖ Judgment belongs to Christ.

Most Brethren Wish To Do Right But Sin Because of Weakness

Even the Apostle Paul felt his human weakness. He pointed out that warfare was being waged within him, between the Spirit of God and his fleshly desires. Because of this warfare, he sometimes failed to do the things he really wanted to do; and at other times, he did the very things he hated. Then, in anguish of spirit he cried out, "Wretched man that I am who shall deliver me from this body of death?" (Romans 7:19-24) Many of our own brethren, perhaps even you, at times have been made to cry the same thing: "Who shall deliver me from this body of death?"

The Apostle Paul hastens to answer his own questions as well as to answer ours. The answer, of course, is Jesus Christ, the Lord. He is the one who will deliver us from this body of death (Romans 7:25). In other words, if we are trying with all of our heart to obey Jesus, His blood will continually wash away our sins (I John 1:7).

Remember that each of us is fighting the same internal warfare; that each of us has his own weakness and besetting sins, and that each of us needs, not condemnation, but all the Christian understanding and encouragement we can get.

Remember, too, since our brothers have weaknesses, we must be careful not to put a stumbling block in their path (Romans 14:13). By creating an occasion for our brother to stumble, we sin against Christ, because Christ died to save our brother and our stumbling block helped to defeat Christ's good work for your brother.

A Few Brothers will be Hypocrites

The word "hypocrite" comes from the mask worn by actors in Ancient Greece. While wearing these masks, the actors pretended to be something they were not. And that's what a hypocrite is: a pretender, a false person; one who pretends to love and obey Jesus. Jesus warned about hypocrites, calling them "wolves in sheep clothing" (Matthew 7:15). And the Apostle Paul warned that false teachers would disguise themselves as Apostles or as an "Angel of light," a preacher (II Corinthians 11:13-15).

How can we tell a false teacher or a false preacher from a true one? <u>Use the famous old Berean recipe:</u> Readily receive the word and search the scriptures daily to see if the things taught are so. Suppose the teacher or preacher is in error, what should you do? Talk to him in <u>private.</u> If he is wrong and really loves the truth, he will publicly correct his error. If he is wrong and refuses to admit it publicly, you may have some room for doubting him. But even that is not proof that he is a hypocrite.

So how can you tell whether a person is or is not a hypocrite? Christ gives us the answer. You will know false prophets and hypocrites by their fruits: Not just because of a <u>single incident,</u> but by the <u>overall pattern</u> of their life. And even then, it is difficult to tell, yes or no, whether they are indeed hypocrites. So to play it safe, don't judge (condemn) them.

Judgment belongs to Christ

There are at least three reasons why we should not judge (condemn) our brother. Here they are:

- ❖ You can't read your brother's heart. Only God can do that. Hypocrisy is not a matter of weakness but a matter of a heart set out to deliberately deceive. Only God can judge motives. Don't try it! (I Corinthians 4:5).
- ❖ Don't judge another man's servant. Your brother does not belong to you. Christ is his master and the only one who should judge him (Romans 14:4).

❖ Don't judge because you yourself will be judged by the same standard you use in judging your brother.

Now suppose that a brother has been guilty of stealing. What should you do? Encourage him to repent. Yes. But suppose he answers you abruptly, "Don't judge me!" How would you answer his defense? Here's a suggestion: Tell him, I am not judging you, the Word of God says, 'Don't steal' (Ephesians 4:28), and when you disobey the Word of God, the Word of God judges you." By doing this, you are not judging your brother but are using the Word of God, hoping to provoke him to love and good works. And that's the right Christian attitude.

THE DEBT OF CHRISTIAN ATTITUDES WE OWE

A great deal of truth was revealed by the poet when he said; "laugh and the world laughs with you; weep and you weep alone." Most people feel they have enough troubles and sadness of their own and are searching for some cheering up, say a happy, smiling face. And joy is one of the right Christian attitudes. Other Christian attitudes include:

❖ Peace.
❖ Humility.
❖ Acceptance.
❖ Empathy.
❖ Kindness.
❖ Forgiveness.
❖ Love.
❖ A prayerful attitude.

Joy

In Philippians 4:4, we are told to rejoice; and in Galatians 5:22, 23, joy is listed as one of the fruits of the Spirit. And even the Apostles went on their way rejoicing after they had been persecuted (Acts 5:41). For at least five reasons we should rejoice. First, we are favored children of the richest, wisest, and most powerful King, who ever existed. Second, this King loved us enough to die for us and to give us all spiritual blessings. Third, this King provides for all our needs (not all our wants, some of which might destroy us). Fourth, the King gives us a well-designed training program with trials to develop us into wise and noble people. And fifth, some day, if we remain faithful, we will live in eternal joy with this great King forever. Can you think of any reason why we should ever stop rejoicing? I can't!

To Peace
Jesus said, "My peace, I leave you." (John 14:27) But what kind of peace did Jesus have? He was contradicted in public, spit on, beaten, and crucified. Does that sound very peaceful? And we are told that if we live a Christian life, we two will be persecuted (II Timothy 3:12). Does that sound very peaceful? Just what kind of peace was Jesus talking about? The answer is peace with God—no aching conscience—because Jesus had completely obeyed his Father in Heaven and had obtained the "peace that passes understanding." (Philippians 4:7).

And that's the kind of peace that we Christians have as long as we live an obedient life. We can live in peace because we know that nothing can separate us from the love of God, nothing now or nothing in the future (Romans 8:35-39). And this glorious assurance brings us both peace and joy.

Humility
One of the seven things which God hates are haughty eyes. (Proverbs 6:16, 17) Solomon pointed out that pride goes before destruction and a haughty spirit before a fall (Proverbs 16:18, 19). Furthermore, we are

told that a lowly spirit will obtain honor (Proverbs 29: 23), that God resists the proud but gives grace to the humble (I Peter 5:5,6) and that we should not take credit for even the good deeds we do (Matthew 5:16, I Peter 4:11).

And what is the human reaction to a person who boasts of himself? Just as much as he enjoys inflating his balloon of pride, so others are inclined to joyfully stick a pin in it. Don't let pride become a challenge to others. It does not make for peace.

Acceptance

Have you ever stood and waited, and waited, and waited while sides were being chosen for a baseball team? Finally, you were the last one to chosen (or maybe not chosen at all). How did you feel? Or perhaps you saw a circle of friends talking; the circle was closed; and no one would allow you to join in the conversational circle. How did it feel? Would you as a Christian wish that on anyone? Of course you would not! So be careful in your acceptance of other people not to rule out anyone. The book of James (Chapter 2) warns us not to be partial but to accept everyone equally, whether rich or poor. And Christ broke down the dividing wall between Jew and Gentile, showing that we should not discriminate because of race or color (Ephesians 2:14). Then, too, God is by nature no respector of persons; so we likewise, as Christians, should show no partiality.

Empathy

"Empathy" means like mind-ness: To experience the exact feelings of another person. We are told to weep with those who weep and rejoice with those who rejoice (Romans 12:15). We are also told to be like-minded the (Philippians 2:2). This of course could refer to either doctrinal unity or our feelings of sympathy. If we truly love one another, we will hurt when they hurt; and often will flow this sympathizing tear.

Kindness

Kindness could be described as <u>gentle thoughtfulness</u>: and it is a characteristic that makes people love us and desire to be with us (Proverbs 19: 22). Kindness has been described as "calling attention to the beautiful flowers beyond the broken gate." It is the characteristic which leads us to point out the praiseworthy; but with great reluctance to call attention to faults, and then only in a way that speaks the truth in love. We are commanded to "Be ye kind one to another tender hearted, forgiving one another even as God for Christ's sake has forgiven you (Ephesians 4:32).

Forgiveness

There are many side roads available to us as we travel on the narrow road to Heaven. Perhaps the widest, most inviting, and deadliest is the one paved with unforgiveness. Once we start down that road, pride may keep us from turning back. Further down that road, we encounter pot-holes, broken glass, other litter and even washouts. But pride may still keep us from turning back, even though the roughness of the road jolts our insides and may even harm our health. What is our destination if we continue on the road to unforgiveness? Referring to our spiritual roadmap (The Bible), we see that this road leads eventually to spiritual destruction if we do not turn back. There to greet us will be the Devil.

The Devil would be a poor host in spite of his making a grand entrée, shish kabob, *from us*; so do we really desire his company? No! One way to escape his company is to R.S.V.P. with such a statement as: I must say no. I do not desire to join your "party." "Witness my complete forgiveness of those who have sinned against me." This, of course, would disappoint the Devil but would prevent you from getting a "hot foot, hot leg, hot arm, etc." So we as Christians must learn to forgive.

What does the Bible say about forgiveness? Jesus had the following to say:

❖ Our Heavenly Father will not forgive our sins if we fail to forgive others (Matthew 6:14,15)

❖ If our brother sins, we are to rebuke him, even if he sins seven times in one day (Luke 17:3,4)

❖ We are to forgive our brother 490 times (in other words unlimited number of times) (Matthew 18:21,22)

❖ We must forgive from the heart: Really mean it when we say that we forgive (Matthew 18:35)

The Apostle Paul, led by the Holy Spirit, also said that we must forgive just as Christ forgave us; and that is <u>completely</u>.

Is it always easy to forgive our brother? No! Not always. But there are three things that can help us. First, we can pray that Jesus will give us strength to forgive and He will do so (Philippians 4:13). Second, we can always use an unusual formula: return good for evil (Roman 12: 21). By doing so, we may make our brother ashamed and may lead him to repent, possibly saving his soul. Not only that but when we return good for evil, it seems to take the sharp edge off our resentment, making it easy for us to forgive our brother. And third, another big help in forgiving our brother is our love for him. Love makes forgiveness easier

Love
The crown jewel of all the Christian attitudes is love. It stands at the head of the Christian virtues (II Peter

1:5-7). It is included in the fruits of the spirit (Galatians 5:22, 23) It is used to describe God's nature (I John 4:16). And God has said that a person who lacks love is <u>nothing</u> even though he:

❖ Speaks like an angel.
❖ Under stands all knowledge.
❖ Has faith strong enough to move mountains.
❖ Give all he owns to feed the poor (I Corinthians 13:1-3)

Love is not a dispensable attitude because it is required by many commandments including these:

❖ The greatest commandment is to love the Lord your God with all of your heart, soul, and mind (Matthew 22: 38)
❖ The second greatest commandment is to love your neighbor as yourself (Matthew 22: 40)
❖ Jesus said that our love should lead us to lay down our lives for each other (John 15:12,13)

Another reason love is said to be so important is because love never fails (I Corinthians 13:8). But what type of love never fails? Romantic type of love (eros) does fail at times because the passion often cools, leading the parties to seek other more glamorous mates. And brotherly love (phila) often fails as disagreements sometimes separate the best of friends. But the love that never fails is the Agape type of love that seeks the highest good of the person loved. It is the type of "tough love" that God shows us when we do wrong; and the peace that passes understanding that He gives us when we do right. It is the type of love of love that provokes us to love and good works.

Would you like to see the Agape type of love described in detail? If so read (I Corinthians 13:4-7).

These verses make a good checklist for measuring our love and determining in what areas, if any, we need to improve. Please read these verses now. We'll wait for you.

We have discussed Christian attitudes at some length. Now, let me point out that our attitudes usually determine what we do and say under any given circumstance. For example, if our attitude is one of love, we will rejoice with a fellow Christian who has received a well-deserved recognition or reward. But if our attitude is one of self-interest, we will probably feel envy when our friend receives recognition. Now, let's reverse our thinking by stating that our actions and words usually indicate the condition of our attitudes (heart) (Matthew 15:19). For this reason, as well as others, we should have our actions and words under our close supervision and control.

THE DEBT OF CHRISTIAN ACTION WE OWE

We owe the debt of Christian example to ourselves, to our fellow Christians, and to the unbelievers of the world. Our actions are important to our brother's salvation. The example we set can either build up or tear down a fellow Christian. And our actions are also important to the unbelievers of the world: Our actions will either draw the unbeliever toward or thrust him from Christ. Let us pray that our actions will never cause any soul to be lost—ours, that of our brother, or that of an unbeliever.

Since our actions are important to our final destiny—heaven or hell—it is essential that we be able to recognize and avoid evil actions and stumbling blocks. It is important that we be able to recognize and take the good actions which should fill a Christian's life. Therefore, this section will cover the following:

- ❖ Avoiding all forms of evil.
- ❖ Avoiding the creation of a stumbling block.
- ❖ Obeying authorities.

❖ Doing good to all men.
❖ Using talents for the common good.
❖ Setting an example for believers.
❖ Setting an example for unbelievers.

Avoiding All Forms of Evil

The Apostle Paul tells us to "prove all things; hold fast that which is good. Abstain from all appearance of evil." (I Thessalonians 5:21, 22) But what can we use to prove all things, whether they be good or evil? The answer, of course, is God's Word, The Bible. Here, again, let me emphasize the importance of Bible study. From Bible study, we could easily catalogue a list of such evils to avoid as:

❖ Adultery (Sexual contact with a married person other than our mate).
❖ Fornication (Sexual contact before marriage).
❖ Uncleanness (Dirty language taking God's name telling unclean jokes).
❖ Lasciviousness (Looking at others to lust after them).
❖ Idolatry (Loving anything more than Jesus).
❖ Witchcraft (Depending upon powers other than God's).
❖ Hatred (A strong dislike).
❖ Variance (Argumentative, not in agreement or accord).
❖ Emulation (Excessive rivalry).
❖ Wrath (Anger in action--it's sinful).
❖ Strife (Contention, fighting, quarrelling).
❖ Sedition (Rebelling against the government)
❖ Heresies (Religious beliefs opposed to the doctrine of the Bible).
❖ Envy (Ill will caused by another person gaining an advantage).
❖ Murder (The premeditated killing of a person).

❖ Drunkenness (Excessive and/or regular use of alcohol).
❖ Reveling (Noisy merrymaking).

This list, though long, may not completely list all evils to avoid. You may discover others as you daily study your Bible. But there is still another category or evils listed: the stumbling blocks. What is a stumbling block? It is any word for action that causes a person to do wrong or to do what they believe is wrong.

Avoiding the Creation of Stumbling Blocks

Please pardon the personal reference which I believe makes the point: While getting my daily two mile walk, I happened to pass a new road kill, a smashed skunk that had already begun to "ripen." The sight and smell were sickening, disgusting. And that pretty well defines "abomination". In the Bible, God declares many things to be abominations, many things that are sickening and disgusting to him. Included are such things as homosexuality, incest, and the sacrifice of children to idols. In addition, in Proverbs 6:16-19, Solomon adds seven other abominations to God's "religious rogue's gallery." Included are these:

❖ A proud look.
❖ A lying tongue.
❖ Hands that shed innocent blood.
❖ A heart that devises wicked imaginations.
❖ Feet that runs swift to mischief.
❖ A false witness.
❖ He that sows discord among brethren.

Not only are these seven sins abominations sinful in themselves but they also act as stumbling blocks leading others to sin.

But some actions or words, though not sinful in themselves may become sinful because of the influence they have on other people: the stumbling blocks they create. For example, the Apostle Paul stated that an idol is nothing, so it was not sinful to eat meat that had been offered to an idol. However, Paul stated he would eat no meat because his example might embolden some of the doubting brethren to eat, thus wounding their conscience, because "he who doubteth is damned if he eats...for whatsoever is not of faith is sin." (I Corinthians 8:9-12, Romans 14:23)

What are the consequences of putting a stumbling block in a brother or sister's way? There are consequences for both the one stumbling and the one who causes the stumble. Because of his sin the brother or sister may be destroyed spiritually. And because of our lack of love, we may stand condemned, especially since we have destroyed a brother for whom Christ died. By doing so, we have sinned against Christ himself.

As you can see, the creation of a stumbling block is a very serious matter. Therefore, we should weigh our actions and our words carefully before we use them. Not only should we ask, "Are they sinful?" but we should ask, "Will it cause my brother or sister to stumble?" If the answer to either question is "Yes," corral those mavericks before they cause a stampede.

Now, before leaving the subject of stumbling blocks, let me ask you a soul-searching question about your manner of dress. "Are your garments too tight or do they show too much skin?" How much is too tight; and how much is too much skin? If your manner of dress is so revealing that it causes members of the opposite sex to have torrid, sexual daydreams, you are wearing your clothes too tight or otherwise too revealing. By doing so, a person could cause a brother or sister to sin (Matthew 5:27, 28). Because you love your brothers and sisters, I don't believe you want to do this.

Now, let's turn our attention to another type of stumbling block: failure to obey authorities.

Obeying Authorities

Disobedience of authority is not only a sin in itself; but it is also a stumbling block that leads to resentment, anger, and other sins. For example, what would be the results if people decided to ignore authority (traffic signals) and attempted to cross the intersection even on a red light? Would this not lead to confusion, resentment, anger, and other sins? And so it is, though perhaps in a more disguised form, whenever rightful authority is disobeyed. Invariably, it serves as a stumbling block for someone.

But to what type of authority are we as Christian's subject? We are subjects to spiritual, parental, work or schools, and civil authorities. Before we discuss each of these authorities let us point out that each of them have been ordained by God himself, and that anyone who resists any of these authorities is guilty of resisting God.

- ❖ Spiritual Authority. Jesus has all authority and has delegated decision about matters of expediency to elders (Matthew 28:18; Hebrews 13:17), pointed out in Chapter V of this book.
- ❖ Parental Authority. "Children, obey your parents in the Lord." (Ephesians 6:1) There is only one circumstance in which a child should disobey his parents: If the parent tells the child to do something that would violate one of God's commands (Acts 5:29).
- ❖ Work or School Authority. "Slaves obey in everything those who are your masters, not with eye service, as men pleasers but with singleness of heart, fearing the Lord" (Colossians 3:22). (If slaves who did not volunteer for their position must do this, how much more

willing to do this should we be who <u>have</u> volunteered for our present position as worker or student?)

❖ <u>Civil Authority.</u> Since God Himself has instituted civil authority we should be subject to it for two reasons: to avoid civil punishment and to keep a clean conscience (Romans 13:1, 5). The laws of the land are to insure that we do no harm to other people.

Do Good to all Men

In Ephesians 2:10, we are told that Christians are "created in Christ Jesus <u>for good works</u> which God has ordained that we should walk in them." Also in James 2:17, 20, we are told that <u>faith without works is dead.</u> This is a very serious matter then since it is our faith in Christ's atoning blood and the resulting obedience that are needed for our salvation.

To further show that this is true, refer to the parable of the judgment scene (Matthew 25:34-36,40); and you will see that the "goats" were condemned for failing to help their fellow man (good works) and the "sheep" were rewarded for helping their fellow man (good works).

Then, too, we are told that he who knoweth to do good and doeth it not to him it is sin (James 4:17). This very well agrees with Galatians 6:20 which tells us to do good to all men, as we have the opportunity.

"Well," you say, "I'm convinced that a Christian must do good as he has the opportunity, but just what kind of good deeds are we talking about?" Good question! Below is a list, short and incomplete, that tells some of the good works that you might do.

❖ Visit the sick or shut-ins.
❖ Feed the hungry or help in the distribution of food.

- ❖ Welcome visitors to church in your age group.
- ❖ Mow widows' lawn or do other handy work.
- ❖ Help janitor straighten up books in the auditorium.
- ❖ Help to move tables and chairs as needed.
- ❖ Help keep the church campus litter-free.
- ❖ Make personal visits to homes of church visitors.
- ❖ Write letters of love and encouragement to sick and to shut-ins.
- ❖ Many other good works as pointed out by church leaders
- ❖ Use your talents to help those either in or out of the Church.

Using Talents for the Common Good

The Good Lord is efficient; he never passes out gifts or talents haphazardly. He gives them for a purpose and intends that they be used when the occasion demands it. According to I Corinthians 12:12-24, each Christian has his own place in the Church, a place no one else can fill and we should use our talents <u>as needed</u> to the fullest of our opportunities (Galatians 6:10), and to the fullest of our ability (Luke 12:48). The failure of any member to do so weakens the Church. With these ideas in mind, let's consider the four following statements that should be made concerning our talents:

- ❖ The use of our talents may at times await the further development of those talents and the presentation of an opportunity. (God has his own timetable.)
- ❖ At the appropriate time, we must either use or talents or lose them (Matthew 25:14-30).
- ❖ To fail to use our talents at the appropriate time is a sin (James 4:17).

- ❖ At any given time, we should use the particular one of our talents for which there is the greatest need. (let's say that you are talented in both teaching and leading songs, you prefer song leading, but the greatest need is for teachers. What should you do? Obviously being an unselfish Christian, you would teach a class wouldn't you? By doing so, you would be setting a good example for your brothers and sisters in Christ, wouldn't you?

Setting and Example for Believers

Someone has said, "What you do speaks so loudly that I can't hear what you are saying." And here is another true statement "actions speak louder than words." Jesus was a master teacher and His sermons are priceless, effective jewels. But some of the most impressive lessons that He delivered were made with actions. For example, Jesus, to teach the lesson of humility, washed the disciple's feet (John 13:4,5); and He set the example of loving service by walking many long and hungry miles for our benefit. Let us never forget these actions that taught us the lessons of humility. And let us not forget that Christ suffered, leaving us an example that we should follow in his steps (I Peter 2:21).

One example, then, that we should set is one of service, lowly service for our brethren, service that say in effect that we "esteem others better than ourselves." (Philippians 2:3).

Other good examples are pointed out by the Apostle Paul in I Timothy 4:12 and include the following:
- ❖ Words that agree with the tone and meaning of the gospel.
- ❖ Conduct that agrees with the meaning of God's commandments.

❖ Words and actions that demonstrate love for God and for our fellowman.

❖ A whole-hearted method of accomplishing all assigned tasks.

❖ Faithfulness in discharging whatever task in God's work that is assigned to us.

❖ Cleanliness in body, mind, words, and actions.

Still other examples that we should set include:

❖ Giving God the credit for any good deeds that we do (Matthew 5:16).

❖ Giving God the credit for prolonging our lives (James 4:13-16).

❖ When volunteers for Church work are requested, be the first.

❖ Be faithful in your Bible study at home, (Your family will notice and you might lead them to Christ by your example.)

❖ Be faithful in your Church attendance. There are many eyes watching a Christian, and your example may lead neighbors to Christ or open the door for studying the Bible with them.

❖ Be neighborly and friendly, but don't be pushy where you are not wanted.

❖ In as much as you are able avoid all sins, especially those of a public nature.

❖ Be quick to confess errors and sins and to make any needed restitution.

❖ Pay your debts, if any, on time, or be thoughtful enough to ask your creditor for an extension of time. (This shows that you are accepting responsibility; and people will thank you for it).

❖ Stay away from places that could give you a bad name or otherwise lead to trouble.

If you set a good example of all the things mentioned here, you will greatly strengthen yourself and your brothers and sisters in Christ. And much of it will also be setting a good example for unbelievers.

Setting an Example for Unbelievers

Most of the good examples which we have discussed for your dealings with believers will apply equally well in your relations with unbelievers. For example, our humble service makes for peace and good impressions where we are employed. Then, too, our good conduct, love of people, and faithfulness in discharging assignments is a credit to us and to Christ in our work situation. And our cleanliness in body and mind, in words, and actions will be favorably noticed by most, but not all of our fellow workers.

To explain: When you leave a circle of fellow employees or ask them not to tell dirty jokes or to take the Lord's name in vain in your presence, you may not be fully appreciated, AT THE TIME! But with the passing of time they will learn to appreciate your standing up for the truth. And later, some of them may even apologize for what they have said in your presence. It has happened!

And finally, here is another good example you can set for your fellow workers: be honest. Don't steal anything, even a pencil (Ephesians 4:28). Don't loaf on the job (Colossians 3:22,23). And use your words to create harmony, not discord. Don't gossip or listen to gossip. When someone comes with an unfavorable report about a fellow worker ask him "how can we help the poor man" (or woman, whoever is the victim of gossip)? This usually will stop the gossip.

And gossip brings us to another debt you owe—Christian words.

THE DEBT OF CHRISTIAN WORDS WE OWE

An old proverb says that "the pen is mightier than the sword." But it is not the sharp point of the pen, the barrel of the pen, nor the ink in it that are so powerful. No! It is the words that the pen writes. The Bible is said to be sharper than a two-edged sword, but the Bible, after all, is composed of words; true, they are very special words, words inspired by God. It is through words that God communicates with us, opens our hearts, and pours his power into our lives. It is through word that we present the Gospel to draw others to Christ. And it is through words that we encourage and build one another up in the most holy faith. But unfortunately, too, it is by words that a person may drive others away from Christ, may tear down and divide the brotherhood, and may alienate fellow Christians. Words are a powerful influence for either good or evil.

A powerful battle of words is constantly in progress because Satan uses words to draw us into sin, to create confusion among the brethren, and to drive unbelievers away from God.

In the words that we speak day by day, whose pulpit are we using – the Lord's or Satan's? Do our words always promote the Lord's cause? Or sometimes does a careless or angry sword deliver a blow that helps our enemy—Satan? We as Christians must closely guard our words, not only because of their influence on other people but also because of their influence on our eternal destiny.

Jesus told his disciples that "on the day of judgment men will give an account of every careless word they have uttered. Then he added: "For by your words you will be justified and by your words you will be condemned (Matthew 12:36,37). He also pointed out that what goes into the mouth does not defile a man but what comes out of the mouth (words) does defile a man.

Is it hard to control your words? Yes! No human being can tame the tongue; it is a restless evil, full of deadly poison (James 3:8). But our religion is worthless if we let our tongue run wild without attempting to control it (James 1:26). So we must constantly strive to master the tongue, trying always to speak the truth in a loving way (Ephesians 4:15). And finally with Christ's help (Philippians 4:13) we will grow in our mastery of the tongue until we make no mistakes with it, well, almost! (James 3:2)

Now that you realize the importance of words and of controlling the tongue, let's discuss some don'ts and do's about the use of words: They will be discussed under the following headings:

- ❖ Don't use words for evil speaking.
- ❖ Use words to teach, warn, and exhort.
- ❖ Use words to confess Christ as Lord.
- ❖ Use words to confess your faults.
- ❖ Use words for prayer and petition.
- ❖ Use words to praise God.

Don't use words for evil speaking
What types of evil-speaking are there? There are at least sixteen types of evil speaking, but several of them fall into closely linked families. Here are the seven familiar ones listed below:

- ❖ Evil speaking caused by discontent.
- ❖ Evil speaking related to anger and its cousins.
- ❖ Evil speaking related to lying and its cousins.
- ❖ Evil speaking related to speaking against something.
- ❖ Corrupt communications.
- ❖ Disputing.
- ❖ Boasting.

Evil speaking caused by discontent

Included in this family of evil speaking are the following:

- ❖ Bitterness, caused by expectations not fulfilled. It is a type of inward, self-inflicted poison that destroys a person and seeps out in all his contacts. Christians should never harbor bitterness, even if they must pray it to death. (Ephesians 4:31).
- ❖ Complaining, sometimes called murmuring, is discontent expressed vocally. When the children of Israel were wandering in the wilderness, many of them were destroyed for murmuring (I Corinthians 10:10). Christians should never murmur (Philippians 2:14).
- ❖ Clamor, is loud complaining and provides the added sin of creating confusion (Ephesians 4:31; I Corinthians 14:33).

This entire family—bitterness, complaining and clamor—have one thing in common: Each of them is based on the belief that the person knows better than God what is needed in a specific circumstance. Thus, each of them implies criticism of God's providence and of God's wisdom. God does not provide all the things we want but only what we really need.

Evil Speaking caused by anger and its cousins

Included in this family are the following:

- ❖ Anger. A person can be angry without sinning (Ephesians 4:26) provided that pride does not prolong anger beyond its natural conclusion or provided that anger does not cause him to commit other sins.
- ❖ Wrath. Anger spilling over into sinful words or actions. Wrath belongs to God;

Christians should not engage in it. (Ephesians 4:31; Luke 3:8)

❖ Rebuke. Rebuke, of course, is sharp criticism, which may or may not be sinful. Christians are told to rebuke vain talkers and deceivers. (Titus 1:10-13). When is a rebuke sinful? When a person strikes out verbally at a brother who has not sinned simply because his pride has been wounded. A rebuke brought about by wrath is unwarranted and sinful.

❖ Railing. Often, when wrath drives a person to give an unjust rebuke, the same wrath may transform him into a "motor mouth," as he raves and rants on and on and on—a railing accusation. Even an angel of God would not even dare to do this (Jude 9).

❖ Malice. Possible that most damaging member of the anger family is malice. This is the serpent of anger, hiding in the bushes and waiting for an opportunity to strike. It is anger in sustained and cowardly forms, and it is fed by unforgiveness, which can cause the person to lose his own soul (Matthew 6:14, 15).

Evil speaking caused by untruth and its cousins

Included in this family are the following:

❖ Lying. Telling something known to be untrue. Not only may a lie damage a person hearing it; but also it does even more harm to the one telling it. Trust is the foundation of all human relations, and truth is completely undercut when a liar has been found our, as eventually he will be. And what could be a worse feeling than to know

154

that our acquaintances completely distrust us? Only one thing: knowing that all liars will have their place in the lake of fire (Revelations 21:8). I certainly don't wish to join them and neither do you!

❖ Guile. Slyness, cunning, and trickery in dealing with other people will eventually be found out. Guile is that form of lying which misrepresents the situation, vocally or otherwise, to gain an unjust advantage. For example, a butcher might press his thumb on the scale to cause the scale to show a heavier than actual weight and then declare, "Yes! Here your are—a full pound!" Christians should imitate Jesus who was completely without guile (I Peter 2:21, 22).

❖ Flattery. Give honor to who honor is due (Romans 13:7) but not unto those to whom it is not due. Don't flatter. Flattery is another form of guile, as the flatterer praises a person not deserving the praise in order to gain an advantage or to cause the persons downfall (Proverbs 29:5; Proverbs 26:28). But the flatterer also harms himself before man and God (Proverbs 28:23; Proverbs 29:5; Psalms 12:3).

❖ Hypocrisy. Hypocrisy means "living a lie"—a person who pretends to be something he is not, or pretends to have feelings he does not have. Can a Christian be hypocritical even in a worship service? Yes! They can. For example, let's say while I was partaking of the Lord's supper "that my mind was on the date I had last night rather than on Christ's great and loving sacrifice. My actions were lying: I was only <u>pretending</u> to have my mind on the Lord's Supper.

For another example: Let's say I am singing "We'll work 'till Jesus comes" but that when I was offered the opportunity, I absolutely refused to do any work of any kind for the Lord. In that case—heaven forbid—I would be a hypocrite, a pretender. Lord, help us always to be <u>real</u>, a real Christian and not a pretender which you, Lord, will condemn (Luke 12:1; Job 27:8).

Evils caused by speaking against

When a person brings an evil report against another human, we call it tale bearing. But an evil report against God, Jesus or the Holy Spirit is usually called blasphemy. Let's briefly discuss each.

❖ <u>Tale bearing.</u> Whether the report is true or not, tale bearing should <u>not</u> be engaged in by a Christian. What harm does tale bearing do? One writer has said that a talebearer is worse than a thief because: "He who steals my purse steals trash, but he who steals my good name does me great harm and does not help himself"

The Bible also points out the harm done by talebearers and includes the following:

- o A talebearer reveals secrets; don't trust them to keep yours (Proverbs 20:19).
- o The words of a talebearer are wounds (Proverbs 18:8).
- o Talebearers keep strife going (Proverbs 26:20).
- o Talebearers prefer talking to working (II Thessalonians 3:10).

156

❖ <u>Blasphemy.</u> As stated before, "blasphemy" means "speaking against," and usually refers to a Divine presence: God, Jesus or the Holy Spirit. What are some of the things that a person can speak against where God is concerned? Here are a few of them:

- o <u>The existence of God.</u> (The fool has said in his heart there is no God. Psalms 14:1).
- o <u>The power of God.</u> (I will do things my way and God can't stop me!)
- o <u>God is a god of darkness.</u> (Gnostic view—Refer to I John 1:5).
- o <u>I can run away from God.</u> (The Jonah view—Refer to Psalms 139:7-12)

Many other examples could be pointed out, but these few should let you see what we mean by "speaking against," blasphemy.

So far we have discussed evil speaking caused by the families of discontent, anger, and speaking against. Now let's turn our attention to other forms of evil speaking, such as corrupt communications, disputing, and boasting.

Corrupt Communications

At times, Job was not a happy man. After losing nearly all of his possessions and all of his family except his wife, Job suffered grievous boils from the sole of his foot to the crown of his head. He was in such pain that he cursed the day he was born. During one of his discourses, Job said, "My breath is corrupt," meaning that his whole life, his whole body was spoiled and rotten. Keep the nasty picture in mind as we discuss corrupt communications, which is just as loathsome and nasty.

What is corrupt communication? It is speech that is contaminated, that is not fit for building up the church.

Included is such vile speech as taking the Lord's name in vain (Exodus 20:7), and telling or listening to dirty (off-color) jokes. Christians are told not to let such corrupt communication come out of their mouth (Ephesians 4:29).

Disputing
It seems that some people are born to argue: their greatest form of entertainment is to dispute. If you say, "gray is an off-shade of white," they will argue, "No! It is a faded shade of black." No matter what, they will find something to argue about. Now, don't misunderstand me; there are times when a Christian should argue: In Jude 3, we are told to contend earnestly for the faith; so if the faith is being attacked, we should draw out our Sword of the Spirit (the Bible) and spring to its defense. But a person who will argue about the Bible facts that do not really matter can be very destructive, especially to a person who is weak in the faith (Romans 14:1). So before a person argues he should ask himself: "Is it important to the truth of the gospel?" If the answer is "No!" then side step any disputes.

Boasting
Let another man praise thee and not thine own mouth (Proverbs 27:2). A self-praising man often causes trouble. He is a challenge to those who hear him; and his boast often leads to conflict. What should a Christian boast about? He can boast about the goodness of God (I Corinthians 1:31). One example of the right type of boasting is the statements made by the author of "Amazing Grace," John Newton shortly before his death. He said, "I remember two things well. First, I am the world's greatest sinner, and second, Christ is the worlds greatest Savior." Now that's the right type of boasting. Boast of our own weakness—Confess our faults—and boast of the goodness of God—honest appreciation.

So far we have discussed the "thou shalt not" use of words. Now let's consider the use of words that a Christian could engage in.

Use Words to Teach, Warn, and Exhort

When asked if he would begin teaching a Bible class, a gifted man replied, "I can't teach. I'm not a teacher," where I pointed out, "John, you have successfully raised four fine children; don't tell me you can't teach." He <u>did</u> become a Bible class teacher, and a good one.

Assuming a person is still alive, each of us does teach daily by words and by example—that's not the question! What are we teaching, and where is it leading those with whom we associate? Are our words and examples leading other people toward or away from Christ? Because of the important influence of our words, like David we should pray:

> "Let the words of my mouth and the meditation of my heart be acceptable in thy sight, O Lord, my strength and my Redeemer." (Psalms 19:14)

Lord, help us always to teach the things that make for love, understanding, and peace. But to do this, we must prepare ourselves to teach, to warn, and to exhort.

Preparing to Teach

Even during our ordinary conversations, if we are to be witnesses for Christ, we must make some preparations, even if limited. For example, if we are leaving a friend with the hope of seeing him tomorrow, we can witness for God's power by saying, "If the Lord will, I will do so and so. Or you can point out, "I won't be able to come tonight, I must study my lesson for Bible Class. (You are not ashamed of it, are you?)

But if you are preparing to teach a Bible class, your preparation must be more thorough as we have previously pointed out in Chapter IV of the book.

Preparing to Warn

Are we responsible for warning others about their sinful condition? If our brother sins, we are to rebuke him (Luke 17:3). We are also told that we are to warn those who are unruly (I Thessalonians 5:14). And we are told by Paul that he warned every man "in all wisdom that we may present every man perfect in Christ."

Before leaving the subject of warning, let me ask this question: If you came home early one morning while your neighbors were still asleep and saw flames springing from the roof of their house, what would you do? Would you think, "Well, it's none of my business and I don't want to get involved. And besides they probably would be angry with me for disturbing their sleep. Is that what you would do? NO! You would warn them that they are about to lose their lives. Should we also warn those about to be destroyed by sin that they, too are at risk (Ezekiel 3:17, 18)?

Preparing to Exhort

What doe the word "exhort" mean? It means to encourage someone to do something, to urge earnestly. We are to exhort each other daily to prevent us from being hardened by the deceitfulness of sin (Hebrews 3:13). We are to patiently exhort (II Timothy 4:2). We are to exhort each other to make supplications, prayers, intercessions, and the giving of thanks for all men (I Timothy 2:1). We are to exhort each other how to walk and please God (I Thessalonians 4:1). We are to exhort busybodies to work with quietness (II Thessalonians 3:11,12). And we are to use sound doctrine to exhort gainsayers to reform (Titus 1:9). Can you complete such exhorting without preparation? No way! Can't be done!

Another type of exhortation we haven't mentioned so far: We should encourage one another to confess Christ by both our words and action.

Use Words to Confess Christ as Lord
Christ said, "Whosoever shall confess me before men, him will I confess before my Father which is in heaven" (Matthew 10:32). Does this mean that <u>once</u> we confess Him in church before people we are <u>done</u> with such confessions? Definitely not! Daily, by words and by actions, our lives should be a confession that Jesus is our Lord.

Use Words to Confess our Faults
The sins and faults of a Christian should never require him to carry on his own private war with the devil. Instead, he should enlist the help pf his loving brethren who can help with prayers and encouragement and who can sympathize, for they, too, are fighting a similar battle. That's reason enough to confess our faults to one another; but there is even a better reason: God said to do it (James 5:16).

Use Words for Prayer and Petition
How would you feel if the President of the United States or the Queen of England gave you a private audience and allowed you to talk at length about anything you choose. Quite an honor! Yes? But even a greater individual than these two has granted you a private audience and allows you to talk as long as you choose about anything you choose. Isn't our loving Heavenly Father nice to us? Isn't prayer wonderful?

Already in chapter 3, we have talked briefly about prayer and we will cover it in greater detail in Chapter X. But here, let me encourage each of us never to down grade the importance of prayer in a Christian's life. It is a great cast used to brace our sin-weakened legs. And it's a great tonic to motivate us to Christian work. And what a bargain: It's free!

Use Words to Praise God

If a bucket brigade tried to put out a fire with buckets without bottoms, how successful do you think they would be? And really that's how successful I feel when I try to use weak human words to give praise to such an all-wise, all-powerful, generous, and ever-loving Heavenly Father.

Or to put it another way, I feel like a child who has learned only how to say "da-da!" And who is trying to proclaim his love for his parents. But if you have ever been a parent, you know that those "da-da's," though far from polished speech, are nevertheless deeply loved and appreciated by you. And I believe that similarly God appreciates our feeble efforts to praise him. When we are full-grown spiritually (only in heaven) then we may find more suitable words of praise than "da-da." In the meantime; Let's keep our praise coming with the knowledge that it pleases our receptive Heavenly Father.

That completes our discussion of your "New Relations With Your Spiritual Family." It has been a long chapter but an important one, because the way you fit into your spiritual family has a lot to do with your happiness here and your preparation for going to heaven. How much have you learned?

To check yourself, work the exercise in "let's See What You've Learned" and "Let's Get Personal."

Section II: Let's See What You've Learned
1. How many brothers and sisters do you have?

_____ When was the last time

that number changed? _____
_____

2. What are four purposes of Christian fellowship?

_____

_____

_____

_____

3. Because there is so much evil in the world, what precautions should Christians observe? _____

_____

_____

_____

4. In what three ways does our attending worship services show our love for Christ? _____

_____

_____

_____

5. What are the five acts of worship?

_____

_____

_____

_____

6. What advantages are offered by Bible study at church? _____

_____

_____

7. How much of our means should be given when the collection plate is passed? _____

_____

_____

8. What is meant by the statement: "Happiness consists of the things that don't own us?" _____

_____

_____

_____

9. What advantages are gained from fellowship in small groups? _____

_____

_____

_____

10. How do you know that God thinks communication is important? _____

_____

_____

_____

11. Give at least five rules that will help to keep communication harmonious. _____

_____

_____

_____

_____

_____

12. What three facts will help us understand why brothers do the way they do? _____

_____

_____

_____

13. If you have heard a brother take the Lord's name in vain and he says, "Don't judge me!" How would you answer? _____

_____

_____

_____

14. For what three reasons should a Christian have the attitude of joy? _____

_____

_____

15. What kind of peace did Jesus leave to us?

_____

16. Why does humility help to make peace?

_____

_____

_____

17. What precautions should a Christian take where acceptance is concerned? _____

_____

_____

_____

18. What does "empathy" mean? _____

_____

_____

_____

19. What is kindness? _____

_____

_____

_____

20. Who does our forgiveness of another person's sin bless? _____

_____

21. How would you rate a man who is a great public speaker, has great knowledge, has great faiths, and given generously to the poor? _____

_____

_____ What factor should your rating depend on? _____

22. Our actions will affect whose salvation?

_____

23. Where will you find the forms of evil listed?

_____

24. How can an action, though not sinful in itself, become a sin? _____

_____

25. How can a woman's manner of dress become a stumbling block? _____

_____

_____

26. Explain why disobeying authorities is not only sinful, but may also be a stumbling block? _____

_____

_____

27. Name the types of authority instituted by God to which you are accountable _____

_____

_____

_____

_____

28. Christians are created in Jesus for _____
_____ without which
our faith is _____
_____

29. List at least 5 types of good works for which you
would now feel qualified and for which you will
volunteer?_____
_____
_____
_____
_____

30. What should determine which of your talents you
should now use for the common good?
_____
_____
_____
_____

31. Name at least six types of example a Christian should
set for believers. _____
_____
_____
_____
_____
_____

32. What should a Christian do if he cannot meet a debt
as scheduled? _____

_____

_____

_____

33. What should you do if you are at a table where dirty
jokes are being exchanged? _____

_____

_____

_____

34. Words can be either a blessing or a curse. Please
explain. _____

_____

_____

_____

35. What defiles a man? _____
And why? _____

_____

36. The Bible says, "No man can tame the tongue," yet it
also says we will be either justified or condemned by
our words. Is this fair? Explain. _____

_____

_____

_____

_____

37. Why are complaining and murmuring such serious
    sins? (Name at least three reasons) _____

    _____

    _____

    _____

38. When should one Christian rebuke a fellow Christian?

    _____

    _____

    _____

39. What causes railing? What is it? And who besides
    men are afraid to use it? _____

    _____

    _____

    _____

40. Which member of the anger family is its cowardly
    form and is most damaging? _____

    _____

    _____

    _____

41. What is guile? _____

    _____

_____

_____

42. When a person uses flattery, what is he trying to accomplish? _____

_____

_____

43. What is hypocrisy? _____

_____

_____

Give at least one example. _____

_____

44. Why does the Bible condemn tale bearing? Give at least two reasons. _____

_____

_____

_____

45. What are two types of corrupt communication?

_____

_____

46. What should determine whether or not one Christian should dispute with another about a Bible fact?

_____

_____

_____

47. What two types of boasts are all right for a Christian to make? _____

_____

_____

48. What did Kind David pray about his use of words?

_____

_____

_____

_____

49. A Christian may use words to teach, to warn, or to exhort.   Which of the three require preparation?

_____

_____

_____

50. How often is a Christian required to confess Christ as Lord? _____

_____

And how does he do it? _____

_____

51. For what reasons should a Christian confess his faults to other Christians? _____

_____

_____

52. Prayer has been compared to a shock absorber, a cast, and a tonic. Please explain why. _____

_____

_____

_____

Section III: Now Let's Get Personal

1. Rate yourself 1-5 on each of the Acts of Worship (1=Best, 5=Worst)

    a. Prayer (leading)

    b. Singing

    c. Bible Study

    d. Observing the Lord Supper

    e. Giving

2. Take your two best and tell how you plan to develop them _____

_____

_____

_____

3. What are some of the things that you now enjoy that you are willing to do without in order to give

sacrificially? _____

_____

_____

_____

4. Rate yourself on the following tips for harmonious communications: (1=Best, 5=Worst)

    a. Slow to speak; quick to hear.

    b. Don't talk too much.

    c. Speak the truth in a loving way.

    d. Praise when deserved but don't flatter.

    e. Don't brag.

    f. Don't gossip

    g. Give God credit for my good deeds.

    Pick out your worst two and work on them; then next worst, etc.

5. Rate yourself on these Christian attitudes (1=Best, 5=Worst)

    a. Joy

    b. Peace

    c. Humility

    d. Acceptance

    e. Empathy

    f. Kindness

g. Forgiveness

h. Love

i. Prayerful attitude

Pick out the two worst and work on them, then next worse, etc.

6. Rate yourself on the following list of evil. Right "YES" before any evil you believe you are guilty of; write "MAYBE' before any evil you are strongly tempted by.

a. Adultery

b. Fornication

c. Uncleanness

d. Lasciviousness

e. Idolatry

f. Witchcraft

g. Hatred

h. Variance

i. Emulations

j. Wrath

k. Strife

l. Sedition

m. Heresy

n. Envy

o. Murder

    p. Drunkenness

    q. Reveling

Pray for strength to overcome your "Yes" and "Maybe" items. Ask a friend to pray with you.

7. List below past examples of your failing to submit to authorities and tell how you have overcome these sins.

_____

_____

_____

_____

_____

_____

_____

_____

8. Rate yourself below on setting these right examples: Put a check mark before each one you have already done and put an X before those you hope to soon do.

_____A. Respond quickly for Church's call for volunteer work.

_____B. Daily study the Bible at home.

_____C. Faithful in Church attendance.

_____D. Be neighborly and friendly but not pushy.

_____E. Avoid all sins of a public nature.

_____F. Be quick to confess sins and faults.

_____G. Pay debts on time or arrange for later
payment.

_____H. Don't go to places that will give church a bad
name.

Plan to work hard to overcome your X's.

9. Rate yourself on these types of Evil-speaking. Use a
check mark to show you are <u>not guilty;</u> use an X to
denote guilt, even occasionally.

  a. Bitter speech

  b. Complaining

  c. Clamor

  d. Wrath

  e. Pouting when angry

  f. Rebuke (without cause)

  g. Railing

  h. Malice

  i. Lying

  j. Flattery

  k. Hypocrisy

  l. Tale bearing

  m. Blasphemy

  n. Disputing

  o. Boasting

p. Guile

Plan a program to overcome all your X-rated items. Your prayers and the prayers of a friend will also help.

Chapter VII. YOUR NEW RELATIONSHIP WITH YOUR PHYSICAL FAMILY

Section 1: Let's Talk About It.

While growing up have you ever been jealous of one of your brothers or sisters, one who you thought had received better treatment than you? If not, you probably are an only child. Jealousy among children is so common that psychologists have given it a special name: "Sibling jealousy."

Perhaps one of the most extreme examples of sibling jealousy recorded in the Bible is that of Jacob and Esau (Genesis 27). Jacob had deceived his father, Isaac, into giving him the paternal blessing highly esteemed during those times. But the blessing rightly belonged to Esau. Was Esau angry? Was his anger fueled by unforgiveness into malice? Yes! Esau planned to kill Jacob as soon as their father died; but Jacob, warned by his mother, Rebekah, fled to escape his brother's wrath.

Normally, sibling jealously does not go this far, but it does cause many problems for parents who must learn to handle it. At times, it requires the Wisdom of Solomon to smooth the troubled waters of inflamed jealousy. So now, you see why children are called a blessing: They keep parents humble and greatly increase their prayer life.

But the parent-child relationship is not the only difficult relationship in the average family: There is also the complex relationship between the husband and the wife—the battle of the sexes, so to speak—that requires a great deal of tact, diplomacy, humility, and love to reach a highly desired "armistice."

In this chapter, we discuss the following:

❖ The duties of the father.
❖ The duties of the mother.
❖ The duties of the children.

❖ The family relationships.

THE DUTIES OF THE FATHER

The duties of the father include those related to family protection and family nourishing. However, he does not perform these duties alone, since the mother ably assists him.

The Protective Duties of the Father

Since the man of the household is usually more physically stronger than the woman, he is often thought to be the protector of the family. This concept dates back to the caveman age when the man, brandishing his club, stood at the door of the cave to protect his family. And even in the Christian age, it was usually the man who went forth to war to promote the safety of the family from an enemy, foreign or domestic.

But do not rule out the protective ability of the wife, who fights like a wildcat when aroused to protect the offspring. Be it husband or wife, either of them would lay down his life for his children (John 15:13).

But what kind of protection do our children need? Protection from physical harm? Yes! We try to provide them with the security of a safe home, with information on the danger of alcohol, cigarettes, and other drugs; with warnings about the dangers of the careless use of automobiles; and with information on the dangers, both physically and spiritually, of sex before marriage.

The Nourishing Duties of Fathers

Before World War II, the father usually was the breadwinner for the family. He earned wages that were used to provide the home and to buy groceries. To a large degree, this has changed, since many women now work outside the home to supplement the family income.

Nevertheless, the husband, to a degree, large or small, still does care for the family finances. But keeping the family's mouths filled with food is probably the simplest part of nourishing the family: Requiring more care and more prayer is the providing of spiritual nourishment.

Who is responsible for the spiritual nourishment of the family? Did you say, "Why, of course, the mother of the family." If so, I have only one thing to say, "Shame! Shame! On the father of the family." It is the father of the family who has been charged throughout the ages and is still charged with the spiritual nourishment of the family, even though the mothers will usually help him. But from 4000 B.C. to the present the father has been assigned the duty of teaching the family spiritually.

Let's go back to the patriarchal age (about 4000 B. C. until 33 A.D.). The father was the spiritual leader of the family. He was the family's prophet, priest, and teacher and was the main link between the family and God. He laid down the rules for the family as he understood them from God. However, the mother of the family helped to teach the children, as shown by Moses' mother teaching him the way of the Hebrew people, even though she was acting as Moses' baby sitter for Pharaoh's daughter (Exodus 2).

Now, let's move forward in time to the mosaic age (about 1500B.C. until 33 A.D.). At the time the Hebrews were told to teach God's commandments to their children, as recorded in Deuteronomy 11:18-20. And as stated in Proverbs 23:22 and Isaiah 38:19, the one chiefly responsible for this was the husband of the family even though the wife probably would help him in doing so.

Note: Even though the patriarchal age started much earlier than the mosaic age, they both existed at the same time from about 1500 BC until 33 AD (the cross). The Hebrews then were under the Law of Moses while the Gentiles were never subjected to that law.

And finally, let's consider the Christian age. Fathers are told to bring up the children in the discipline and instruction of the Lord (Ephesians 6:4) But not to provoke your children to anger (Colossians 3:21). This means that fathers are to teach the truth in a loving, gentle way to the children; yet they are to discipline the children as required to mold them toward obedience.

Note: Since the father of the family usually has a full time job, when he is available to teach the Word of God to the children? He can do so under several circumstances. For example, he can hold daily devotionals at breakfast or at the night meal. Or while he and the children go on a walk, go camping, or go to a ballgame, he can bring applicable verses from the Word of God into his conversation.

What are the main duties of fathers? Here they are:
- ❖ To provide for the family's physical needs. To fail to do so when possible is to deny the faith (I Timothy 5:8).
- ❖ To teach his children the way of the Lord.
- ❖ To provide a Christian example for his children and his wife.

In all of these duties, the husband receives help from his wife.

THE DUTIES OF THE MOTHER

The duties of the mother, like those of the father, include ones related to the protection and nourishing of the children. In addition, the mother usually serves as a beautifier, comforter, mediator, and social secretary.

Women seem to have more highly developed tastes for beauty than men. They love pretty clothes, pretty interior decorations, pretty flowers and pretty poetry. Although men usually lack the good taste possessed by women, they do appreciate the final product. Girls, your husband will enjoy the flowers you grow. And that is part of your job. To add beauty.

Women, too, seem to be more highly developed as comforting agents. When a child has skinned a knee or suffered some other "boo-boo," like a homing pigeon, he will head straight for his mother. A kiss then eases the pain (whether this is local or general anesthetic, I don't know. But it does work.) So keep puckered up for the boo-boos, girls.

Women, too, seem to be skilled at mediation. Men seem to be more bent on justice; while women seem to be more merciful by nature. Interacting together, the parents seem to come out with a more reasonable form of discipline. But don't misunderstand me: <u>When necessary</u>, a woman can hand out discipline as tough as any Army Sergeant. (Believe me! I know.)

Women, too, usually need to serve as the social secretary of the family, for at least two reasons: First, they are usually more skilled socially than us men. And second, one person in charge tends to prevent embarrassing conflicts, for example, when a husband and wife accept a dinner invitation, FROM DIFFERENT PEOPLE.

Before leaving the duties of women in a family, let me point out this word of warning: <u>don't make your husband a whipping machine:</u> Don't tell Junior. "Just wait until your father gets home; he will give you a hard whipping."   If Junior needs a whipping, you do it. Otherwise, you place the husband in Junior's enemy camp and destroy his influence with Junior.

And now let's talk about Junior, what can we say about him?

THE DUTIES OF CHILDREN

The duties of children are to appreciate, love, honor and understand their parents. In many instances these four overlap; but here we will discuss them separately.

Appreciate our parents

Some poet has said, "How sharper than a serpent's tooth is a thankless child." Indeed it does sting when we as parents do our best to help a child and find that our best is not appreciated. Usually, a person cannot fully appreciate what their parents have done for them until they have children of their own. Then they know! But you are smart: begin today to appreciate you parents for all they have done for you. How many sleepless nights have they spent to help ease your earache, toothache or high fever? How many tears have they shed and how many prayers have they pleaded for your benefit? How can you fully repay your parents' love? Only by passing it on to your own children. But we can appreciate our parents and tell them so now. Their tears of joy may flow!

Love our parents

Jesus said, "If you love me, you will keep my commandments" (John 14:15). And this is one way we show our love for our parents: By obeying them. We can also convince our parents that we love them by showing thoughtfulness when they feel tired or ill, and by volunteering to perform such needed chores as making the bed, washing the dishes, taking out the trash, or mowing the lawn. The fact that you volunteered will really give your parents a thrill. Then too, when our parents get old and feeble, how can we show love? By doing what we can to take care of them.

Honor our parents

How can you honor your parents? By telling them how much you love and appreciate them? Yes! But there are other ways. One of the ten commandments is to Honor your father and your mother so your days upon the earth will be long (Exodus 20:12). Why will honoring your parents <u>lengthen</u> you life? Because dishonoring your parents may <u>shorten</u> your life. In Exodus 21:17, parents are instructed to put to death any child that cursed them; but this commandment was under the law of Moses and is not enforced today. What, then, do we mean that to dishonor our parents will shorten our lives? Suppose we rob a bank? Will that dishonor our parents? And we could be killed during or after the robbery. Then, again, suppose we commit murder. Will that dishonor our parents? In what ways could that shorten our lives? Or suppose we frequent a beer-joint where fights regularly break out. Would this honor our parents? And could it possibly shorten our lives? Perhaps now you understand why to honor your parents can lengthen our lives.

Understand our parents

"Why my parents won't let me use the family car on my date. I'm already twelve years old and I know I could drive just as good as dad. I think they are being selfish and thoughtless about the car. And I do need it to impress my girlfriend."

Of course, you would never think such thoughts, would you? No, you would not, because you understand that your parents are trying to protect you from harm.

"Why would anyone think such thoughts," you ask. The answer is that many times some people are driven by the "I-want-it-so-badly complex," a complex that completely clouds their otherwise good judgment. In such cases, the parent with more experience and cooler judgment recognizes the dangers involved and makes decisions that protect the child. At such times, the child must try to understand why the parents act as they do, although lack of experience and "I want it so badly" do make it difficult for the child to do so.

What are some of the adult decisions that a child must try to understand? Here are a few:

❖ Be home by 10:00 p.m. (Most of the trouble people get into occur after this time.)

❖ You can't buy a toy like your friends have now. Later perhaps (The rent and utilities are due and the supply of money is short).

❖ You can't have a chemistry set for Christmas (We see how careless you are and we don't want you to burn the house down).

❖ You can't play until you mow the lawn (You must learn to work and to accept responsibility).

❖ You are grounded for one week (He who does not discipline, hates his own son: Proverbs 13:24. Whom the Lord loves he punishes: Hebrews 12:6. And so do godly fathers).

Now that we have spoken at length about the duties of fathers, mothers, and children, let's tie all these facts together more closely by seeing what the Bible says about family relationships.

FAMILY RELATIONSHIPS

In Ephesians 5:28-31, we see that because of love, a man and woman shall be joined as one flesh as husband and wife. The joining of the flesh is soon accomplished, but the joining of the pairs' thoughts, actions, and spirit is time consuming, perhaps requiring a lifetime. After all, the marriage relationship is complex and is beset with many problems. But before we discuss these problems areas, let's get a bird's eye view of the marriage relationship.

The General Framework of Marriage

Someone has pointed out that God did not form woman from Adam's head so that she should rule over him. And God did not form her from Adam's feet so she should walk all over him. But instead God took woman from Adam's rib, near the heart so that man should love her.

And this is spelled out, using different words with the same meaning, in Ephesians 5:24-31. From these verses we see that man is the head of the house, but that his love will lead him to be open-minded toward his wife's ideas and opinions. We also see that man must love his wife as much as himself. No selfishness here!

If the husband does love the wife, how will he treat her? His love will lead him to treat her as given in I Corinthians 13:4-7 which includes:

- ❖ Be long suffering (be patient with her).
- ❖ Being kind (showing gentle thoughtfulness)
- ❖ Don't envy the wife's success.
- ❖ Doesn't brag to show his "superiority" over the wife.
- ❖ Treat wife with politeness.
- ❖ Doesn't always seek his own way or advantage.
- ❖ Doesn't question the wife's motives.
- ❖ Doesn't rejoice at wife's failures (instead he sympathizes).
- ❖ Rejoices with wife at her successes.
- ❖ Patiently endures wife's failures and excesses.
- ❖ Refuses to accept gossip reports about wife.

Now, let's flip the coin over. How should the wife treat the husband? Exactly the same as he treated her: with love.

Now that you have the general framework of the marriage relationship in mind, let's briefly consider marriage problem areas.

Marriage Problem Areas

Included in marriage trouble areas are those related to understanding and communications, forgiveness, kindness, the raising of children, the use of money, and the selection of leisure-time activities. Let's briefly discuss each of these problem areas.

Understanding and communication

Once there was a man who spoke only German who was engulfed by love at the first sight of a girl who spoke only Chinese. Since she at once returned his love, the two were married by a preacher who spoke only English. "Ridiculous!" you say and I agree, but it does make the point that understanding is highly to be desired in marriage.

Even if the bride and groom both speak English, will each of them speak in a way that the other can easily understand? Not always! In my opinion, there are some basic differences in the way that men and women think. Some reasons I have for believing this are as follows:

❖ Women Place Stronger Emphasis on Love. Someone has said, "To a man, love is a hobby; but to a woman, love is her main occupation." Women do seem to place a stronger emphasis on things related to love. And this emphasis on love leads to a more highly developed social skill than most men have. Included in this social skill is tact.

❖ Women Are Usually more Tactful Than Men. Men often take the direct route and plunge headlong into a conversational area "where angels would fear to tread." Women are usually more subtle, and talk around the point so that other women catch the idea with less pain. Meanwhile, a man overhearing their conversation hears <u>only what has been said</u> while the woman hears <u>what was meant.</u> Later, the wife may translate the conversation into male terms.

❖ <u>Women Have a Wider Range of Concentration Than Men.</u> We men are a great deal like a horse with blinders: We think in a narrow but intense range, suitable to say, for scientific research. But a woman seems able to concentrate well on a wider panorama, making her suited for acting as a hostess at a party or for raising children. As an example, too, I have heard three women talking <u>at the same time;</u> yet when the conversation was finished, each could tell you what the other two had said. Could a man do this? Never! Our range of concentration is narrow.

I believe that men and women understand and communicate in slightly different ways and that we must learn how to communicate using the other sex's system. This takes time, patience and forgiveness.

The Problem of Forgiveness

A hermit who lives in a cave, without any human contact, is not apt to hurt anyone's feelings. The more contact we have with other people, the more chances we have that things will go wrong, that misunderstandings will take place and feelings will be hurt. And where will you find more personal contacts than between husband and wife?

What should a husband or wife do when their mate has hurt their feelings? Swallow hard and say nothing? No! The injured party should speak the truth in a loving way and say, for example: "Honey, what you said hurt my feelings. Did you really intend to do that?" Hopefully, such a loving complaint will be the start of working out the difficulty. This line of action is better than silently resenting little things until they grow into major problems.

The Problem of Kindness

"That's about the dumbest thing that I ever heard you say. You've said some dumb things before but this is the stupidest." Do you think such a statement would help to produce harmony in a marriage? Is there anything wrong with such a statement or perhaps I should ask is there anything right about it? By examining the statement more closely, we can see that there are at least three things wrong with it.

First, the statement is not spoken in a loving way. It is harsh; it is biting, and is delivered as a rebuke to one who has not sinned. Therefore, the very tone of it is sinful. We are to speak the truth (Is it true?) in a loving way (Is this loving?).

Second, the selection of words is very insulting. Notice the words "dumb" and "stupid." Has the one speaking followed the Golden Rule (Matthew 7:12). Would he like to have these words applied to him? I think not! So, again, this statement is sinful.

And third, the statement dredges up things from the past which should have been already forgotten. It seems that the victim of this statement is being forever reminded of her real, or supposed, shortcomings. Perhaps next, the accuser will remind her of the errors she used to make while learning to crawl. Love does not rejoice at the shortcomings of others, but in kindness tries to hide them.

What effect does real kindness have upon a marriage? Proverbs 19:22 states that the kindness of a man makes him to be desired. This is also true between husband and wife. The kindness of each makes them desire each other's company more and more. While the unkindness if practiced for long, will tend to separate husband and wife, at least spiritually. Be ye kind one to another, tenderhearted, forgiving one another, even as God for Christ's sake has forgiven you (Ephesians 4:32).

The Raising of Children
In our neighborhood there lives a man who is very strict on his children; to counteract this, the mother hid the wrongs of the children from him and would not punish them herself. What were the results? There was constant friction between the man and his wife concerning the raising of the children. But worse yet, the children were ruined. One of them shot his younger sister; and the other girl was rather a "wild onion." In fact the other girl's husband threatened to kill her if she did not stop "running around."

Failure for the parents to agree on the methods for raising children can harm both the marriage union and the children. It is important then for the parents to agree and to present a "solid front" to the children. Otherwise, the children will play one parent against the other in order to get their way. Our children tried this—ONCE! If mama had said "No" and they asked Daddy, the result was a spanking, an automatic spanking, no questions asked, no excuses tolerated. Children are smart. They learn fast.

Here's another line of reasoning children sometimes use on parents when their request has been refused, "But Daddy, everybody's doing it." The reply: "You are wrong! Not everybody is doing it! You are not. And anytime you tell me "everybody is doing it" the answer is an automatic "NO". They never used that line of reasoning again.

Do parents sometimes disagree on the type of punishment for a given offense? Yes! But don't disagree before the children. Work it out in private—usually a compromise—to present the "solid front" to the children.

But children must be punished in some way for the wrong they do; however, the punishment must fit the "crime." The punishment can be one of light pain, a kind talking to, boredom, or withholding of rewards. Speaking of light pain: If you bust them in the right place, they won't break, but it may put a brake on the undesired action. With some children, a kind talking to will break their heart worse than a razor strap. But by far one of the most effective punishments for children is boredom. A child by nature is active and any lack of activity, such as going to their room, standing in a corner, or counting beans will bore them to tears. In fact, one of my children begged me to whip him instead of having him count beans. And of course, there is the punishment of withholding rewards: "Since you have done wrong, you will not be allowed to ride your bike for a week."

Before leaving the punishment of children, let's ask this question "What does God say about it?" Proverbs 13:24 states that "He that spareth the rod hateth his son." Children must be disciplined either by their parents or later by the state. This, however, can become a bone of contention if parents are not willing to make a Christian compromise. The same is true of the use of money.

The Use of Money

He wants! She wants! The children want! And sometimes there is not enough money to satisfy everyone's wants. Who is going to be pleased and who is going to be disappointed? Can you see the possible grounds for conflict here? How can we solve such a dilemma; where are you, Solomon?

Here's a suggestion: First, point out to your family that God tells us to pay all our debts (Romans 13:8). Then, list what if anything, you owe along with the bona fide

<u>needs</u> of life (not wants, but needs). Next, list the cost of each item. (Does this sound like budgeting? Good!) Then, subtract from your total income the amounts needed for debts and bona fide needs. If nothing is left over, your problem is solved: Nobody gets money for their "wants." But suppose that $50.00 is left over; who gets it? In family conference, decide how the $50.00 should be divided. Let's say that the children get $5.00 a piece; the parents get $10.00 apiece and $20.00 is reserved for emergency money. (Emergencies will come.) The children will grumble a little but not as much as if they had no part in the decision-making. And while solving this problem you were training your children in taking financial responsibility and in budgeting, both of which will serve them well in later years.

The Use of Leisure Time

Johnny wants to go play baseball; Susan wants to go watch ice-skating; Daddy wants to go fishing; and Mama wants to go to the ballet. Mama also wants the family to enjoy their leisure time together! Here again, we see grounds for conflict. What is the solution? Something has to give!

Here again, I suggest using a family conference to work out who does what and when. The solution will probably consist of a series of more or less reluctant compromises; but at least everyone will know that their wants have been seriously considered.

So much for our discussion of physical family relationship. Have you learned a great deal? Let's see. Answer all of the questions in Let's See What You've Learned.

Section II: Let's See What You've Learned

1. What is sibling jealousy and why is it a problem for a
    family? _____

    _____

    _____

2. What are the two main duties of the father of the
    family? _____

    _____

    _____

3. How can a father fulfill his duty to nourish his children
    spiritually? _____

    _____

    _____

4. In what ages has the father been responsible for
    teaching his children about their relationship with God?

    _____

    _____

    _____

5. Besides helping the father perform his duties, what
    other duties are the responsibilities of the mother?

    _____

    _____

    _____

6. Why should the father and mother reach a compromise
    on the administration of discipline for the children?

_____
_____
_____

7. How can you fully repay your parents' loving sacrifices
   for you? _____
   _____
   _____

8. Why does honoring his/her parents help to lengthen the
   life of a child? _____
   _____
   _____

9. In what ways can you honor your parents?
   _____
   _____
   _____

10. Why does a child have difficulty in understanding why
    a parent sometimes refuses to honor his request?
    _____
    _____
    _____

11. Why does it take so many years before a husband and
    wife can become joined in thoughts, action and spirit?
    _____

_____

_____

12. What is the significance of God forming Eve out of Adam's rib and not some other member of the body?

_____

_____

_____

_____

13. Where will you find a detailed description of how a husband should treat his wife; or vise-versa?

_____

_____

_____

14. Why do women usually have more highly developed social skills than men? _____

_____

_____

15. What is meant by the statement that women are usually more tactful than men? _____

_____

_____

16. Why are women usually better as party leaders than men? _____

_____

17. What should a husband or wife do when their mate has hurt their feelings? _____

_____

_____

18. What effect does unkindness have on a marriage?

_____

_____

19. When a mother and father disagree on the type of discipline needed, why should the compromise be reached outside the children's hearing? _____

_____

_____

20. What does God have to say about the punishment of children? _____

_____

_____

21. What problems can arise because of the use of money? And how should they be solved? _____

_____

_____

_____

_____

22. What type of punishment should be used where one particular child is concerned?

_____

_____

23. What problems can develop because of the use of leisure time; and how can you solve them?

_____

_____

_____

24. What advantages can result from family conferences to solve problems? _____

_____

_____

Section III: Now Let's Get Personal

1. How would you overcome the urge to be jealous of a brother or sister? _____

_____

_____

2. Knowing what facts should increase your trust in the warnings and information your parent's give you?

_____

_____

_____

3. What can you do to increase the trust of your parents?

    _____

    _____

    _____

4. What would be your reaction to a devotional brought by
    your father at the night meal? _____

    _____

    _____

    _____

5. How can you increase your reception of such a
    devotional? _____

    _____

    _____

6. Who had you rather discipline you, your mother or your
    father; and why? _____

    _____

    _____

7. Do you complain more about what you don't have, or
    do you express thanks more about the things you do
    have? _____

    _____

    _____

8. How long has it been since you expressed appreciation
    to you mother and father for the things they have done

for you? Don't count Mother's Day and Father's Day.

_____

_____

_____

9. In which ways have you recently brought honor upon your parents? _____

_____

_____

Dishonor?

_____

_____

_____

10. Does wanting something badly affect your judgment in making a decision? _____

_____

_____ How can you prevent this from happening? _____

_____

_____

11. What is your attitude toward a parent when he has disciplined you? _____

_____

_____

12. On the next page are items based on the characteristics of love which you should have for family members. In the columns that <u>apply to your situation</u>, rate your behavior toward each family member in each of the characteristics. Put a check (√) for satisfactory and (X) for unsatisfactory.

<u>CHARACTERISTIC</u>	<u>FATHER</u>	<u>MOTHER</u>	<u>SIBLINGS</u>
Long-suffering (Patient)	_____	_____	_____
Kind	_____	_____	_____
Avoiding the feeling of envy	_____	_____	_____
Avoiding bragging	_____	_____	_____
Polite	_____	_____	_____
Don't insist on having own way	_____	_____	_____
Don't question motives	_____	_____	_____
Don't rejoice at failures	_____	_____	_____
Rejoice at others successes	_____	_____	_____
Patiently endure failures and excuses	_____	_____	_____
Refusal to accept gossip	_____	_____	_____

For each of the items rated (X), how do you plan to improve? _____

_____

_____

13. When your feelings are hurt by a family member, how do you usually react? _____

_____

_____Do you think this reaction should be improved, and if so, how? _____

_____

14. Write below on the left some unkind statements that you have made in the last year; and on the right, write the way you think they could be reworded to make them kinder.

1._____   _____

2._____   _____

3._____   _____

4._____   _____

5._____   _____

NOTE:
If more than five spaces are required, use the blank space below VERSES TO MEMORIZE.

VERSES TO MEMORIZE
Ephesians 6:4   Exodus 20:12   Proverbs 13:29

Chapter VIII. YOUR NEW RELATIONSHIP WITH THE WORLD AND WORLDLINESS

Section 1: Let's Talk About It.

Have you ever gone fishing all by yourself just to get away from the clamor and hubbub of day-to-day living? How great it was, as a change of pace, to just sit and meditate—or maybe snooze—while hearing the gentle rush of the water and watching the float on your line bob lazily up and down.

Or perhaps at times, you have gone on a nature hike alone to relax and enjoy the beauty of God's creation and to marvel at the beautiful picture God has painted for your enjoyment in a glorious sunset. How great the change of pace seemed! But would you really like such solitude as a "regular diet"? I think not.

But there was a religious group in the time of Christ, called the "Essenes," who did follow a life of isolation from the world. *Have you ever heard of them? Few have.* They lived apart from the world in monasteries in order to escape the sinful pollution of the world. To their credit, the Essenes believed in living a life of complete obedience of God's commands, unmixed with human opinions. Sounds good! They believed what Christ believed: obey God. But there was one important difference between Christ and the Essenes: Christ moved among people to do good; the Essenes lived alone to escape evil.

What did Christ say about living apart from the world? John 17:15 records that Jesus said, "I pray not that thou take them out of the world but that thou should keep them from the evil one." Christ always had good reasons for anything he said; but in my human thinking, I can see these two reasons for Him making His statement:

❖ While living in isolation, we could not influence the world for good and consequently the ever-present evil would make things go from bad to worse.

❖ While living in isolation, we cannot develop the strength of character that should grow in us with the passing of years. For this reason, James 1:2-4, points out that we should rejoice when we have been tempted and have overcome it because we then are developing steadfastness.

Why does meeting and overcoming trials and temptations produce strength of character? Let me use this illustration to explain: In Texas, where the winds are usually constant and sometimes fierce, a newly planted pecan tree is whipped savagely by the wind which tend to break it or to tear it from the ground. This continues until the tree is grown. And what is the result? Because of the buffeting wind the tree develops rugged strength and can safely withstand winds of 60 miles per hour, or higher.

Now, let's shift geographically to the Philippines, where the winds usually do not blow. Since the trees are seldom whipped by the wind, they do not develop strength and are easily shattered by typhoon winds even weaker than 60 miles per hour.

Be thankful, therefore, for your trials and temptations. By overcoming them, you develop spiritual strength—but only if you do overcome them.

In this chapter, we discuss the world and worldliness. Included are the types of temptations we have, the type of trials we have and the help we have in overcoming them.

MAN VERSUS TEMPTATIONS

Why is man tempted and what are the types of temptations? To answer the first question, man is tempted because his nature exposes him to the three avenues of temptation. The answer to the second question, the types of temptation, will be covered later in this chapter.

The Three Avenues of Temptation
In John 2:15,16, the Apostle John warns us not to love the world neither the things of the world. If we do love the world, he states that the love of God is not in us. John then points out the three following avenues of temptation:

❖ The lust of the flesh.
❖ The lust of the eye.
❖ The pride of life.

Why is each of these called an "avenue?" Because an avenue is a broad street and the road to destruction is a broad one. And each of these three is a broad, well-traveled street.

What is the first Bible example of sin caused by following these three avenues? The answer concerns Adam's wife Eve. Eve had been told not to eat of the forbidden fruit, but because of Satan's lie and the three avenues of temptation, Eve was tempted. She found that the fruit was good to eat (lust of the flesh), that it was pleasant to look at (lust of the eye), and that it would make one wise (pride of life). Thus, because of Satan's lie and the three avenues of temptation, Eve disobeyed God and brought sin and death into the world.

Are those three avenues of temptation open to traffic today? Yes! They are freshly paved and very well traveled. How do these avenues tempt us today? Let's look at man's nature to see why we are so tempted by these avenues today. Here goes:

❖ <u>Lust of the Flesh.</u> We desire to experience pleasure from our sense of taste, touch, smell, and hearing. Down this avenue, come such sins as gluttony, the use of drugs, sex outside of marriage, and listening to music so loud that it damages our sense of hearing.

❖ <u>Lust of the Eye.</u> We want to see things pleasant to the eye; for example, beautiful clothes, pretty furniture, etc. The enjoyment of beauty is not in itself, sinful. But when the love of beauty causes us to give less to the Lord than we have purposed in our heart, then we have, in effect, robbed God (Malachi 3:8, 9).

❖ <u>The Pride of Life.</u> When we desire some honor strong enough to sin to obtain it, we have stumbled down the avenue of the pride of life. For example, to defeat a rival running for the same office, a politician might spread false tales about him, thus sinning.

Now that you have the avenue of temptation in mind, let's discuss the types of sins brought about by these temptations.

The Types of Sins

Included in the types of sins are sinful thoughts, sinful words, and sinful actions. Can thoughts be sinful if we do not follow through with sinful words or sinful actions? Jesus said so in Matthew 5:22, 28, 44 and 45. Can words be sinful? Yes, if they are harsh ones, lies, or otherwise cause pain or trouble. And of course, we know about sinful actions. These sins: thinking what is evil, saying what is evil, and doing what is evil are called the "sins of commission," something we have committed.

But to complicate things, these are also "sins of omission," leaving unthought, unsaid, or undone some of the good things we have the ability and opportunity to do. As pointed out in James 4:17, "He who knoweth to do good and doeth it not, to him it is sin." Also the Apostle Paul points out that we are created in Christ Jesus for good works (Ephesians 2:10) and that we should do good to all men, especially to them of the household of faith (Galatians 6:10).

Now, bearing in mind that the Devil is a sly opportunist, where do you think that he is most likely to attack a Christian? The weakest point of all is sins of omission. If the Devil can keep us from thinking, saying, or doing something good, he has a foot in the door and can soon get us to sin more and more. First comes the sin of omission of failing to think the good thoughts, with this sin we have laid the foundation for other sins. After all, if we are truly grateful for what God has done for us, we will, in appreciation, fill our lives with good works to "redeem the time because the days are evil." (Ephesians 5:16) One of our strongest defenses against Satan is to keep busy doing good because "Idleness is the Devil's workshop." Of course, there are other helps which we will discuss later in the chapter.

But now, let's get a little more specific by listing some of the things pointed out as sins in the Bible.

Specific Sins Pointed Out in the Bible
During the days of the Apostle Paul, a group of people using human "logic," came up with the most peculiar idea: they taught that since God's grace covers our sins, let us sin more and more so that God's grace will abound. The Apostle Paul might have thought: "Oh! No! What will they think of next?" And Paul did not hesitate to point out the error of their "logic."

In Romans 6:1-6, Paul pointed out that in baptism we had died to sin and that we should no longer serve sin. Then in Romans 6:17, he pointed out that if we serve sin, we have become servants of sin rather than servants of God. Can you think of a vivid example of a person who has become a servant, no a slave, to sin? You might think of a drug addict, but there are many others.

We as Christians are under King Jesus and the perfect law of liberty. We must be careful not to disobey our King, lose our freedom and become a slave to any type of sin. What are the types of sins? We have mentioned them once before in the book, but please allow us to list them again for emphasis. Most of these types of sin are given in Galatians 5:19-21 and include:

- ❖ Adultery (Sexual contact with a married person other than our mate).
- ❖ Fornication (Sexual contact before marriage).
- ❖ Uncleanness (Dirty language taking God's name in vain or telling unclean jokes).
- ❖ Lasciviousness (Looking at others to lust after them).
- ❖ Idolatry (Loving anything more than Jesus).
- ❖ Witchcraft (Depending upon powers other than God's).
- ❖ Hatred (A strong dislike).
- ❖ Variance (Argumentative, not in agreement or accord).
- ❖ Emulation (Excessive rivalry).
- ❖ Wrath (Anger in action--it's sinful).
- ❖ Strife (Contention, fighting, quarrelling).
- ❖ Sedition (Rebelling against the government)
- ❖ Heresies (Religious beliefs opposed to the doctrine of the Bible).
- ❖ Envy (Ill will caused by another person gaining an advantage).
- ❖ Murder (The premeditated killing of a person).

❖ Drunkenness (Excessive and/or regular use of alcohol).
❖ Reveling (Noisy merrymaking).

Each of these sins results from an <u>inward test</u> as man is tempted by means of three avenues of temptation. But not all tests come from inside a person. Some tests come from the outside and are called trials.

MAN VERSUS TRIALS

Jesus was tempted in all ways as we are, yet without sin (Hebrews 4:15). But did He also receive trials just as you and I do? Yes! And more so. How many of us have suffered such trials as the following:

❖ Walking many long and weary miles.
❖ Being falsely called an illegitimate child (Luke 3:23; Matthew 1:18; John 8:41).
❖ Being contradicted during teaching.
❖ Being called the Son of the Devil.
❖ Being exposed to guile in question form.
❖ Being spit on in public.
❖ Being falsely accused at a mock trial.
❖ Being weakened from a lack of sleep and food.
❖ Being stripped naked in public.
❖ Being mocked with a crown of thorns.
❖ Being publicly beaten.
❖ Being crucified.

You and I will probably never suffer such extreme trials as Jesus; nevertheless the Apostles, you and I have all been promised persecutions. In Matthew 10:17-25, Jesus told the Apostles that they would be persecuted; and in II Timothy 3:12, the Apostle Paul stated that each of us would be persecuted if we lived a Godly life in Christ Jesus. And that is a promise! What kind of persecutions will Christians get in this modern world? Well, we probably

will not be thrown to the lions; but here are some of the
types of persecution we might receive:

- ❖ The loss of a friendship because we will not
  bend to peer pressure and join in the sinning.
- ❖ Being called a religious fanatic or "goody-
  goody-two-shoes," or some other offensive
  term.
- ❖ Being called a troublemaker when others
  falsely testify against us.
- ❖ The loss of popularity with the "wrong
  crowd."
- ❖ Envious gossip by those we make feel guilty
  of their sins.
- ❖ The loss of job advancement because of
  false accusations.

Probably we could add more to this list, but enough
has been said to show that we as Christians will receive
trials and persecutions.

When we receive persecutions, how will we react?
Well, there are two possible courses of action. We could
"cave in" to peer pressure and to the desire to please other
people. The Apostle Paul warns us against this in Galatians
1:10 when he stated, "If I yet pleased men, I would not be a
servant of Christ." And there you have it: Either pleases
man or God. And pleasing God is your second possible
course of action: Stand firm! Do you know what is right?
Withstand the consequences and reap the reward!

What reward does a Christian receive for obeying
God when being persecuted? There are many, but let me
list a few of them here:

- ❖ Rejoicing that we have been counted worthy
  to encounter persecution for Jesus' sake
  (Acts 5:41).
- ❖ Development of patience and steadfastness
  (James 1:2-4).

❖ Experiencing the peace that passeth understanding (Philippians 4:7).
❖ Receiving a crown of life (James 1:12).

But before we can wear the crown, we must first carry the cross (Matthew 16:24). And those trials and persecution are just like splinters on the cross, so to speak, that painfully gouge our flesh. Is it easy to withstand trials and persecutions? No! And at times it seems that we are too weak to bear it ALONE.

HELPS AVAILABLE DURING TEMPTATIONS AND TRIALS

As a Christian you do not have to bear any burden alone. Instead, the sources of help available include God, Jesus, the Holy Spirit, and fellow Christians. From these sources we get the following types of help:

❖ A way of escape provided to prevent us from sinning (I Corinthians 10:13).
❖ Strength that comes from Jesus (Philippians 4:13).
❖ Comfort and help as we read the Bible.
❖ Comfort and help from fellow Christians (Galatians 6:2).

That completes our discussion of the new relationship of a Christian with the world. To see what you have learned, work the exercise titles "Let's See What You've Learned" and "Now, Let's Get Personal."

Section II: Let's See What You've Learned
1. What disadvantages come form living the life of a

hermit? _____

_____

_____

2. What did Christ say about his disciples withdrawing from the world? _____

_____

_____

3. What advantages are gained from meeting and overcoming trials and temptations?

_____

_____

_____

_____

4. The three avenues of temptation are

_____,

_____, and the

_____

5. When did these avenues first lead a human into sinning? _____

_____

_____

6. Give an example of the lust of the flesh.

_____

_____

7. Give an example of the lust of the eyes.

_____

_____

8. Give   an   example   of   the   pride   of   life.

   _____

   _____

9. In what three general ways can a person commit a sin?

   _____, _____

   and _____

10. In what three general ways can a person sin by
    omissions? _____

    _____ and

    _____

11. What does the Apostle Paul mean by the statement:
    "Redeeming the time because the days are evil?"

    _____

    _____

    _____

12. Why is this statement wrong? "Since Gods grace
    covers our sins, we should sin more and more so that
    God's grace may abound." _____

    _____

    _____

13. How   can   we   become   slaves   to   sin?

    _____

    _____

    _____

14. What is the difference between a temptation and a trial?

_____

_____

_____

15. What types of trials are a modern day Christian likely to face? _____

_____

_____

_____

16. What types of help are available to a Christian during his trials? _____

_____

_____

_____

Section III: Now Let's Get Personal

1. What type of sin is your besetting sin (hardest to resist)? _____

_____

2. How do you plan to conquer this sin?

_____

_____

_____

_____

3. What type of sin have you already conquered?

_____

_____

_____

4. What is the next type of sin you plan to conquer?

_____

_____

_____

5. Describe one occasion when you were tempted by each of the avenues of temptation and tell how you overcame it.

      a. Lust of the flesh: _____

_____

_____

_____

      b. Lust of the eye: _____

_____

_____

_____

      c. Pride of life: _____

_____

_____

_____

6. Tell one sin of omission you have experienced since becoming a Christian. _____

_____

_____

7. Describe one trial you have had after becoming a Christian and tell how you should/did overcome it?

_____

_____

_____

_____

Chapter IX. YOUR NEW RELATIONSHIP WITH
WORDLY AUTHORITIES

Section 1: Let's Talk About It.

A young boy, joyfully playing in a neighbor's yard, has just been told by his sister, "Mother wants you to come home, <u>now.</u>" But since the boy strongly desires to play longer, he can think of all sorts of false reasons for disobeying his mother. For example, these thoughts might cross his mind:

❖ Mother probably did <u>not</u> really send sister.
❖ Mother was just joking.
❖ Mother really didn't care very much or she would have come herself.
❖ Mother probably has forgotten about sending sister by now.
❖ Sister seemed very happy in spoiling his fun; so just to put sister in her place, he won't go home.

In much the same way, too, we are still tempted, as we grow older, to dream up false reasons for doing things <u>the way we want to do them,</u> rather than submitting to authority. Here are a few examples of some grown up, but still false, reasons for disobeying rightful civil authority:

❖ Speed limits are <u>not</u> for us good drivers but are intended for <u>poor</u> drivers with weak eyesight and poor reflexes.
❖ Stop signs help poor drivers avoid accidents but us good drivers can check intersections while driving through them at 30 miles per hour. So there's no need for us to stop.
❖ I've got excellent reflexes; I can tailgate all I want to—safely.
❖ Using turn signals to turn or change lanes is too much trouble and anybody who can't see

that I intended to change lanes is just too blind to be driving.
❖ When I want to back up, you should stay out of my way.

These sorts of false reasons are cheerfully provided to us by the Devil who loves to color and corrupt our thinking. To prevent the Devil from clouding our thinking about civil authorities, let's discuss the true source of government authority, the requirement for obeying civil government, the requirement for obeying work and school authorities, what disobedience costs you and me, and the requirement to obey higher-than-government authorities.

THE TRUE SOURCE OF GOVERNMENTAL AUTHORITY

In a democracy such as ours, it is commonly stated that governmental authority comes from the consent of the people being governed. Does Romans 13:1 agree with this statement? According to that verse, what is the true source of all government authority? The answer, of course, is God. This makes disobedience of civil law a more serious offense.

"But the laws are made by wicked and corrupt politician who often takes bribes": you say, "I don't respect them so why should I obey laws of an evil government."

GOD GRANTS AUTHORITY TO ALL SORTS OF GOVERNMENT

God has several reasons for granting civil authority even to wicked nations. For example, he granted power to Pharaoh of Egypt so that God could show his power to the world (Romans 9:17). For another example, he granted Pilate (of an evil government) power, we know, because

Jesus told Pilate: "Thou could have no power against me except it be given from above" (John 19:11). For a third example, God raised up some evil nations to punish Israel for their sinning. So you see: whether civil governments are good or evil, they are raised up to accomplish the purposes of God.

THE REQUIREMENT FOR OBEYING CIVIL GOVERNMENT

Why should a Christian obey the laws of the land? Here are five good reasons:
- ❖ To keep a clear conscience: Disobedience is sinful and should pain our conscience (Romans 13:3-5).
- ❖ To escape punishment: God will impose it through his representatives in civil government (Romans 3:3-5).
- ❖ To prevent our example from being a stumbling block for other Christians (Romans 14:13).
- ❖ To prevent bringing disgrace on the church.
- ❖ To prevent weakening our Christian influence in our efforts to lead others to Christ.

What laws of the land should we obey? First, let me point out that we are to obey, not judge, the laws of the land. What does it mean "to judge the laws of the land?" There are at least two ways that we might be guilty of judging the law. For example, turn back to the introduction of this chapter and notice the first five examples related to the laws governing the use of automobiles. In each case, the driver has judged that the law did not really apply to him.

Another way we can judge the law is to decide that some part of the law applies to us but that other parts do not. For example, we might decide that the law related to vehicle registration should be obeyed but the law on vehicle inspections should not. If so, lots of luck! Pay your fine with cheerfulness.

Always remember that all laws and all parts of each law are included for our observance, whether the law deals with automobiles, taxes, or revenues.

Obeying the Tax Laws

Even though the mention of taxes may send a sharp pain coursing through the nerve that connects our hearts to our pocketbooks, we really should pay all taxes cheerfully. (Did I hear a loud "Boo"? No! Really I mean it!) We should cheerfully pay our taxes for two reasons.

First, taxes in the United States of America are the biggest bargain you can get these days. Just think of the presence of law enforcing officers—city, county, state and federal—available for your protection. (Some of the countries I have visited require that we hire guards because of the weakness of protection from law enforcement officers). Then, too, remember protection from fires. Our fire departments carry on excellent training programs on fire prevention, respond rapidly if our house catches fire, and also responds rapidly to keep your neighbors house, when aflame, from setting your house on fire. And let's not forget the department of public safety which helps to train drivers and who enforce safe driving on our highways. These are but a few of many reasons that I say that we should cheerfully pay taxes.

Another reason for cheerfully paying taxes is that Jesus said to do so in Luke 20:22-25, Jesus said, "Render unto Caesar the things that are Caesars" (tribute or taxes; verse 22). And in Matthew 17:24-27, we read that Jesus caught a fish that had money in its mouth and then used the money to pay taxes.

NOTE: NO! NO! NO!
You can't tell the IRS to wait for your taxes until you catch a fish with all your tax money in its mouth. They might get impatient.

In paying income tax, for example, is there a difference between self-preservation and honesty? Yes! If we do right for fear of being caught and punished for doing wrong, that's self-preservation. But if we do right even when we know that we won't be caught while doing wrong, that is honesty.

On one classic TV program, the law enforcing officers were ridiculed and called "revenuers," while the bootleggers were glorified. How sad! How unfortunate! How sinful to glorify sin! God has told us to pay revenue when due; and any evasion is sin. So a Christian should never patronize a bootlegger, nor should he cross a state line in order to reduce or evade paying revenue. Tax evasion is tax evasion and revenue evasion is revenue evasion, no matter how we color the picture.

So far we have considered obedience to civil authorities. Next, let's broaden our discussion by considering obedience to work and school authorities.

REQUIREMENTS FOR OBEYING WORK AND SCHOOL AUTHORITIES

What does the Bible say about work and school authorities? Several things. First, Romans 12:17 says to provide things honest in the sight of all men. This rules out thievery, large or small, and the stealing of time (loafing), whether or not the boss is watching. Then, too, Ecclesiastes 9:10 also rules out loafing or deliberately slowing down on the job when it says, "Whatever your hands find to do, do it with thy might." And Colossians 3:22,23 tells slaves to "work heartily as serving the Lord." This statement was addressed to slaves who might or might not have volunteered for the job. How much more strongly should this apply to an employee who <u>has</u> volunteered to do the work?

By the way, we should work heartily as serving the Lord because in any job that we do we are indeed working for him: Our Christian example during work will reflect favorable or unfavorably on our Master, Jesus and on the Church. Not only that but bad work habits and crime, on or off the job, can be very costly.

WHAT DISOBEDIENCE OF AUTHORITIES COSTS YOU AND ME

In a talk at a Toastmaster's Club, I passed around a beautiful purple wastebasket and asked each member to put $5,000 in the basket. Needless to say, I did not get any money: but I did get their attention, just as I hope that I now have yours. I then pointed out that stealing, vandalism, loafing on the job and taking unnecessary sick leave costs the <u>average American family</u> $5,000 per year. (This approximation was carefully calculated after phone calls with a local Better Business Bureau.) How can we stop or reduce this needless expense? Here are a few suggestions:

- ❖ Make certain that none of us is guilty of such wasteful sins. (I don't think any of you are guilty).
- ❖ By example and words, discourage dishonesty and other failures to observe work authorities.

NOTE: Incidentally, the school environment resembles the work environment and everything said about the work environment also applies at school.

So far, we have stressed the fact that we should always obey civil government. But is there an exception to this rule? Is there a time when a Christian <u>must</u> disobey the law of the land? Yes! If there is a conflict between civil authority and the higher authority.

THE REQUIREMENT TO OBEY HIGHER-THAN-GOVERNMENT AUTHORITY

Did Jesus and the Apostles ever fail to observe the dictates of civil government? The answer is "Yes!" Jesus never disobeys even one of Gods commandments but he did disobey one of the traditions instituted by man. As recorded in Matthew 12:10-13, Jesus healed a man with a withered hand on the Sabbath which was against man's traditions but showed God's loving nature.

Then, too, there are two instances where the Apostles disobeyed the rulers in order to obey God. Peter and John said they should listen to God rather than man (government, Acts 4:5, 18-20). And Peter and the Apostles said they should obey God rather than man (Acts 5:27-30).

But now, let's flip over the coin to see what government-granted rights that a Christian cannot in good conscience make use of. Here are some of them:

❖ Divorce except for adultery (Matthew 5:31,32; Matthew 19:3-9).
❖ Lawsuits against a fellow Christian (I Corinthians 6:1-7).
❖ Free speech if we mean gossip, lying, and cursing.
❖ Pornography and/or dirty jokes.

How much have you learned about our obedience to worldly authorities? Work the exercise "Let's See What You've Learned" to find out:

Section II: Let's See What You've Learned
1. What is the true source of governmental authority?

___

2. Why does God grant authority to evil governments?

_____

_____

_____

3. Why should Christians obey the laws of the land?

_____

_____

_____

4. What is meant by the expression "judging the law?"

_____

_____

_____

5. How do you know that God favors the paying of taxes?

_____

_____

_____

6. To set a Christian example, what are some things that we should avoid doing on the job? _____

_____

_____

_____

7. How would you describe a Christian example of a conscientious worker? _____

_____

_____

_____

8. What type of words and actions should a Christian exhibit while attending school? _____

_____

_____

_____

9. What unchristian actions can increase the cost of the things we buy? _____

_____

_____

10. When is it acceptable to disobey the laws of the land?

_____

_____

_____

Section III: Now Let's Get Personal

1. In the space before each listed item, rate yourself on your observance of laws. Put a checkmark for the item you always obey; put an "X" before the item you never obey; and put an "S" before the item you sometimes obey.

    _____ Carefully observing all speed limits.

    _____ Observing all stop signs.

_____ Never tailgate another car.

_____ Always use turn signals before making a turn.

_____ Always use turn signals for changing traffic lanes.

_____ Give other traffic the right-of-way when backing up.

_____ Observe "yield" signs, giving other traffic the right-of-way.

_____ Wait patiently for your turn at 4-way Stop Sign.

_____ Never judge the laws of the land.

_____ Never try to evade taxes and revenues.

_____ Never steal on the job or at school.

_____ Never commit vandalism.

_____ Never loaf or slow down on the job.

_____ Never abuse the use of "sick leave."

2. With prayerful determination work to improve on any item you noted "X" or "S" in the list above.
3. Verses to memorize:

    Romans 13:1

    Romans 13:7

    Romans 14:13

    Ecclesiastes 9:10

Chapter X. YOUR NEW RELATIONSHIP WITH PRAYER

Section 1: Let's Talk About It.

What is required for the physical body to grow? At least five things: food, digestion, rest, motivation and exercise.   Without food—perish the thought—the body soon dries up and dies. Without digestion, our food cannot nourish our body. Without rest, the body cannot repair itself. Without motivation, the body vegetates and loses zeal for action. And without exercise the body will atrophy and lose strength and stamina.   Now each of these statements is probably no surprise to you; you have known each of them for a long time.

But did you know the same five requirements exist for spiritual growth? To grow we must have spiritual food, regular feasts on the Word of God.   As recorded in Matthew 4:4. Jesus has said, "Man does not live by bread alone but by every word that proceeds from the mouth of God." Then, too, in John 6:63, Jesus pointed out that the words that he spoke were spirit and life. And in I Peter 2:2, we are told to desire the sincere milk of the word that we may grow. (By the way, how often do you feed the physical body? How often the spiritual body? Think about it!)

To continue living a Christian life we must also have exercise—the doing of good works for which we were created in Christ Jesus (Ephesians 2:10).   Otherwise our faith will die (James 2:17), we will deceive ourselves, we will soon forget what we have learned, and we will not receive the blessings of God (James 1:22-25).

So far we have discussed the requirements for spiritual food and exercise. How do we meet the rest of the requirements for growth? The answer is "by prayer."

THE ADVANTAGES OF PRAYER

Prayer is helpful in at least three ways: digestion, rest and motivation. Each of these three is needed in the life of a Christian.

Prayer Aids Digestion

Have you ever eaten a delicious meal only to discover later that you had developed heartburn or some other form of faulty digestion? Can the same thing happen to us when we eat spiritual food? Yes, it can! To prevent spiritual indigestion, we should make use of a digestion aid—prayer. Before beginning a study of the Bible, we should pray for wisdom to understand the truths that we are in most need of <u>at our present level of Christian development.</u> If we pray earnestly, believing, God will answer such a prayer because it agrees with his will (II Timothy 2:15). And it is comforting to know that God will not criticize us for asking for help (James 1:5).

Prayer Gives Rest

One thing we all have in common is problems. They come in assorted sizes and types. There are big problems, little problems, once-in-a-lifetime problems, and problems that seem to come back over and over again.

Some of these problems, we can easily handle. Other problems we can handle with great difficulty. Still other problems require the help of our Christian friends. And there are other problems so complex and difficult that we are consumed by worry and remorse that no one seems able to help us solve them. They may haunt us day by day and even parade across our sleepless pillow at night. Then, we know that we must seek help more powerful than humans can provide. Upon realizing our helplessness, we turn to the Bible and to prayer: our conversation with God.

In reading God's Word, we find that we should forsake our worrying (Matthew 6:31-34; Psalms 37:4,25) and that we should make our requests known to God (Matthew 7:7). His shoulders are broad and He can handle the problem for us. As God shoulders our troubles, we feel release from worry, added strength, and incentive for doing God's work.

Prayer Provides Motivation

Prayer changes things. Sometimes it changes our circumstances. In other instances, prayer changes our attitude and gives us a jolt of spiritual energy that motivates us and sends us to work for God. Sometimes the work is a job we have known about for a long time but have hesitated to start until prayer sensitized our conscience. At other times, our eyes are opened to an important work that we have never thought about before. But regardless of whether the work is new or old, prayer is a powerful "pry" that moves us out of our state of "do nothing."

Now that we have discussed the powerful advantages of prayer (digestion, rest, and motivation) let's turn our attention to some general principles concerning prayer, and the right address for prayer.

A Definition of Prayer

One common definition of prayer is "to address God, telling Him what is needed or wished." Even though this definition is true, it is far from complete. It leaves out the elements of glorifying and worshipping God, a necessary ingredient of prayer, as pointed out in our later discussion of the "Model Prayer." But before we cover the Model Prayer, let's cover other general principle of Payer.

The Right Time for Prayer

Since we are to pray without ceasing (I Thessalonians 5:17), anytime is the proper time for prayer.

If we have the right attitude, (more about that later) it does not matter, morning, noon, or night; each time is the correct time for prayer. But perhaps some explanation should be given about the statement "pray without ceasing." If you are leading public prayer, and if you have prayed for 30 minutes, the auditorium would probably be either filled with some very indignant people—preacher included—or be completely empty. *A prayer doesn't have to be everlasting to be eternal.* Pray without ceasing means to pray regularly, no skipping days, and to pray often each day: Morning upon rising, before each meal, at night when you return to your family from work, and at night before retiring. At other times, we should be in such a prayerful mood that the slightest hint of a feeling of gratitude for God or *the slightest hint* of a problem would touch our hair trigger and explode us into prayer. Our life as a Christian should never lead us far away from a prayerful mood.

Are there circumstances that will "kill" our prayerful mood, circumstances that we should, if possible, avoid? Yes! Being in the wrong place for a Christian, listening to the wrong type of talk, or developing Unchristian feelings. The wrong place is any place that leads to evil thoughts, for example, "X"-rated movies. The wrong talk is dirty jokes, and the wrong feelings, for example, is anger which can cloud our thinking. After all, we cannot lift prayerful hand to God while our fists are clenched.

The Right Position for Prayer

What is the right position to be in while praying? Kneeling? Standing? Lying on your back? Lying on your face? Hands together? Hands raised to God? Head bowed? Face raised to heaven? Just what is the right position for Prayer? <u>Any position</u> is the right position for prayer and can be supported by Bible examples. Even if you are standing on your head in an overturned car with water pouring in, <u>that</u> is the proper position for prayer—and my! Would you need it!

Actually the right position for prayer is not one of physical body position but rather one of having our <u>attitude</u> in the right position—on the straight and narrow and "on the level' with God.

The Right Attitude for Prayer

One thing that usually will insure failure in any undertaking is having the wrong attitudes. This is always true in our prayer life: the wrong attitude will always insure failures. But what are the right attitudes? They include respect, gratitude, faith, the right motives, and importunity.

- ❖ <u>Respect.</u> Should we respect God, our all-wise and generous Heavenly Father, the one with the power to shorten or prolong our lives, the one who can grant or refuse our requests, and the one who has already given us life, breathe, and all the blessings, that we now enjoy? Because of God's power and goodness and because of our love for Him, we should "fear God and keep His commandments" (Ecclesiastes 12:13), thus showing our respect for Him during prayer as well as at all other times.

- ❖ <u>Gratitude.</u> We should feel genuinely grateful for what the Lord has done for us at all times but especially during prayer. Our expression of gratitude to God is one form of worship; and we should be <u>honestly</u> profuse in our expression of thanks to God, Jesus and the Holy Spirit. They have done so much for us. Our gratitude is a small but well-appreciated repayment to them.

- ❖ <u>Faith.</u> In three senses, we should show faith in our prayers. First, we should pray according to <u>the faith,</u> the will of God: we should never ask for anything that would be sinful for us to possess. By doing so, we are asking God to be an accomplice to our sin, very insulting to our Heavenly Father who can never be tempted to sin (James 1:13). Second, we should believe that our request will be granted by God; otherwise we will not receive our request (James 1:6,7). And then, we should ask with faith in the goodness of our Heavenly Father: that He will refuse to give us anything that would be harmful to our soul. After all, He is a good Father.

❖ The Right Motives. Prayer should be unselfish! We should pray for the benefit of others as much, or more than, we should pray for our own benefits. And we should never pray for things that will help us to sin or to continue in sin. Such prayers will be answered, "No!" (James 4:3). One example of a prayer to be answered, "No!" A little boy sat crying and praying on the curb, afraid to go home because he was due punishment. His prayer: "Please dear God, hide my father's razor strap." A selfish prayer and one not for the boy's benefit. If he escaped punishment, he would probably continue to misbehave.

❖ Pray with Importunity. There's the story about the young man who proposed to the sweetheart but she said, "No!" Leaving despondent, he never asked her again. If he had only known: the next time she would have said "yes!" Does God sometimes invite us to ask over and over again before he finally says "yes!" to our prayers? Reading Luke 18:2-6, we see that God encourages our importunity (our keeping on keeping on in prayer) until we finally get what we want. Why does God want to be asked over and over again before He grants some requests? Because of His pride or stubbornness? No! By delaying His answer, God could be testing our earnestness, how badly we really want something.

Or our request could have come at a time not beneficial for our own best interest, so God wisely delayed His answer to a more appropriate time. (For example, consider the prayer of a seven-year old boy who prayed for a real automobile and a gun that would shoot real bullets. Overhearing his prayer would his earthly father grant him either of his requests? Not if he loved the boy! And remember that God loves us, too!)

The Right Address for Prayer

If you tried to send a letter to Aunt Martha in a blank envelope, would she get it? No! Your letter would lack two things: an address and a postage stamp, representing the authority to mail. Well, a prayer needs the same two types of ingredients. It needs an address—our Heavenly Father (Matthew 6:9) and it needs a grant of authority to permit its travel—The Lord Jesus (Matthew 28:18; John 14:13). There you have it: the address and the "stamp." We pray to God in the name of Jesus. But remember "in Jesus name" means "by the authority of Jesus." So we had better be careful to pray only for those things that Jesus would truly approve of.

And speaking of Jesus, He not only authorizes our prayers now, but while on earth, He gave us direction on how to pray, called the Model Prayer. And the model is useful for private and public praying.

THE MODEL PRAYER

The model pray is sometimes (in error) called "The Lord's Prayer." There is one very good reason that the outline for prayer, given in Matthew 6:9-13, cannot in truth be called the Lord's Prayer. In verse 12, we ask God to forgive us our debts (sins) as we forgive our debtors (those who sin against us). But Jesus committed no sin (Hebrews

4:15); so He could not pray that his sins be forgiven, and therefore it could not be His prayer. Notice, too, the purpose for which the model prayer was given. The disciples had asked Jesus to teach them how to pray (Luke 11:1). His reply was to give the model prayer (Luke 11:2-4). So this was not the Lord's prayer but a model used to help His disciples learn to pray. And even today, it still serves well as a fill-in-the-blanks type model for prayer.

The Elements of the Model Prayer

Jesus never spoke or acted haphazardly. The same is true of the model prayer: each of its parts was given for a purpose. Let's see what the purpose of each element is.

Our Father Who Art in Heaven

This element identifies which father we are talking about—Our Heavenly Father not our earthly one. In effect, it is a pledge of allegiance to God, recognizing that He has the authority of the father of our spiritual family and that we, His children, owe Him our loyalty and our obedience. Can we in good conscience pray this part of the prayer if we do not intend to obey Him? To do so would be hypocritical and would dishonor our Heavenly Father.

Hallowed Be Thy Name

This line of the model prayer, I believe, has two distinct meanings. The word "hallowed" means "holy" or "sacred." Can we truly pray this line if we habitually take the Lord's name in vain? (Exodus 20:7). No! By taking the Lord's name in vain, we have made it common, not holy.

Another possible meaning of "hallowed be thy name" is "you are in a class to be honored far above us humans." In this sense in our prayer, we point out how God is the creator; how good and merciful is His nature, how He provides for us, His children, and how He is worthy of our praise.

Thy Kingdom Come
Jesus taught the model prayer <u>before his death and the establishment of the church</u> (29-33 A.D.). But looking at Matthew 16:18,19, the kingdom and the church seem to be the same because they are used interchangeably. Since the church now exists, we should now pray, "Thy kingdom grow," which fits in nicely with the next line of the model prayer.

Thy Will Be Done On Earth As It Is In Heaven
It is easy to imagine that in heaven there is love, unity, peace, and complete obedience to all of God's commands. And this line of the prayer asks that the same love, unity, peace, and obedience will develop here on earth. I do not need to point out that these conditions do not yet exist on earth; so you can see that we Christians face some rather hard challenges.

Give Us This Day Our Daily Bread
This line of the prayer requests the necessities of life: food, clothing, and shelter. But notice that the prayer is <u>for daily</u> bread (the necessities) and not for jam and marmalade (luxuries). Do we as Christians have a right to pray for luxuries (things we want but don't really need) when there are far too few missionaries in foreign lands and the ones we do have may be poorly supported? (That's food for thought, isn't it?)

Forgive Us Our Debts (sins) As We Forgive Others
Christ's precious blood cleanses us from sin, but it cannot do its job if we hold a grudge, malice, or ill will against any person (Matthew 6:15). But you say, "I won't

forgive that person unless he first asks for my forgiveness." If this is your attitude let me ask you this question: are you going to let your salvation depend upon another person's repentance? Isn't that rather risky? I certainly would not do that! Instead I should go to my brother and work things out (Matthew 18:15-17).

But suppose our brother has sinned against us seven times, shall we forgive him? Yes! Seventy times seven times we are to forgive him (Matthew 18:21,22). Does this mean that when he sins 491st time that we are free to lower the boom? No! Jesus is using figurative language which really means to forgive him each time he sins, regardless of how many. Wow! Would that require great spiritual strength? Yes! But Jesus can give it to us (Philippians 4:13).

Lead Us Not Into Temptation

This line is really asking God to keep us from being exposed to trials and temptations that are too strong for us and to provide us a way of escape so we can bear the temptation (I Corinthians 10:13).

Deliver Us From Evil

God can deliver us from evil in at least two ways: providing a way of escape (already mentioned) or give us strength to overcome the trial or temptation (Philippians 4:13). To obtain the needed strength to overcome some trials we might have to spend time in very earnest prayer. But we can win the battle!

For Thine is the Kingdom, Power, and the Glory

This element of the model prayer is not an after thought; it is, I believe, a kind of summation of the other eight elements "thy kingdom come" and "thy will be done." Included in "thine is the power" are the four elements "give us our daily bread," "forgive our sins," "lead us not into temptation," and "deliver us from evil." And included in "thine is the glory" are the two elements "our Father in Heaven" and "Hallowed be thy name."

By now, you should understand the elements of the Model Prayer, so let's apply them to your private prayer life.

The Model Prayer's Aid to Private Prayer
Since our private prayers are known only to God and ourselves, we usually make them detailed and intimate. So let's take the model prayer line-by-line and supplement it to make it more personal.

Our Father Who Art in Heaven
What are your personal feelings as we approach God in prayer? Are we feeling love, dependence, respect? If so, say so. Are we feeling particularly happy, grateful, or saddened and discouraged by a problem? If so, say so. Our God already knows what's in our heart, but he wants us to express it in words, for our own benefit. Putting our feelings in words helps to untangle our thoughts and increases our closeness to God.

Hallowed Be Thy Name
In this part of the prayer, we praise God for His power, grace, and providence. We express to God the honest compliments that we feel in our heart. Don't try soft soap! God can read our hearts and will be disgusted by any phoniness. We should speak the truth in love as we feel and believe it in our hearts.

Thy Kingdom Come, or rather Grow
What things will help God's kingdom to grow? If we are trying to persuade a friend to become a Christian, we should now earnestly pray for him, mentioning him by name. And we should pray that the work of preachers,

elders, deacons, and other church members should prosper, helping to lead others to Christ. Then, too, we should pray for the recovery of the sick, by name, so they will be returned to their place of duty. Also remember those that need comfort because of the loss of a loved one. After comfort, they may also be available to strengthen the Church. And don't forget to pray for the leaders of our country that their decisions will also help God's kingdom to grow.

Thy Will Be Done on Earth

We pray that we may be grown closer to the perfect pattern set by the Lord Jesus Christ while here on earth. We pray that our words and actions will promote love, peace, unity, and obedience to God's every command. We pray that our lives will encourage others to grow in love and good works. And we pray that this same prayer will be answered in the lives of other Christians.

Give Us This Day Our Daily Bread

We pray that God will give us what we really need in the way of food, clothing, and shelter. If our car is about to die a timely death and if we need it for transportation to work or to school, we can pray for another car. But don't pad the account! If the old car is still serviceable and dependable, live with it a little longer. Ask only for what we actually need not for what we merely want. And pray the same prayer for fellow Christians if you know of their bona fide needs.

Forgive Us Our Trespasses

Here, we get very personal and very specific: "God help me to forgive Theophratis for pouring syrup in my car seat. He meant it as a joke, but what a mess! Especially when I sat down in it! And God, please forgive the lustful thoughts on my mind when Terpsichore walked by. I should have turned away at once but I enjoyed watching her. So please forgive me, Lord." As you can see, this is a very intimate part of the prayer, known only to the person and God.

Lead Us Not Into Temptation
Here again, we get rather personal and intimate: "Lord, help me not take revenge on Theophratis by putting a dead skunk in his car. And help my neck to be limber so I can look the other way when Terpsichore walks by." This part of the prayer resembles a father-and-son talk.

But Deliver Us From Evil
Here, we pray for wisdom to see the way of escape in order to avoid losing the battle against temptations and trials. We also pray for strength to meet these problems. We describe to God our problems, trials, and temptations. And spell out the type of aid we are requesting. Here again we get very personal and very detailed.

For Thine Is the Kingdom, Power, and Glory
Here, we tell God that we are aware of His supreme power and goodness, thereby showing our own humility. We infer or state plainly that we are lost without His help and ask God to answer our prayers.

In Christ's Name We Pray
Lord, though your blood and high position you hold beside God, please plead our case so that our prayers will be answered.

Amen! So be it!

The Model Prayer's Aid to Public Prayer

Before discussing the line-by-line use of the model prayer as an aid in leading public prayer, let me make three points that set the stage for discussion.

First, leading public prayer is difficult! Why? Well, have you ever seen a person riding two horses at the same time in a circus? Leading public prayer compares well with that act. We are addressing a sincere and worshipful prayer to God (Here we ride one horse). And we are trying to influence the audience to follow our lead while filling in the blanks with their personal details (The second horse). Unfortunately, too, we usually do not have as much practice before the performance as the circus rider does.

NOTE: Immediately before leading a public prayer, I always pray privately that God will help me lead a public prayer that will be pleasing to Him, glorifying to Jesus, and edifying to the Church. And it does seem to help me a great deal.

Second, there is a difference of opinion on whether a public prayer should be written before hand or read without even notes. The opponents say that a written prayer is not as sincere as one lead without notes. I personally do not agree with that statement. Sometimes, under the pressure of leading public prayer—riding two horses, remember—our thoughts get tangled up and we say things we honestly did not intend to say. Is that sincere praying? Remember the audience has heard the unintentionally insincere remarks and is so bewildered that their prayer thoughts is interrupted.

On the other hand, to prepare a written prayer shows we have taken seriously our task in leading public prayer and that we sincerely want to say the right thing. Not only that, but given abundant time to meditate, we can say exactly what we mean, especially if we are careful to speak the truth in love, avoiding phoniness and flattery, or anything else that does not come from the heart. As you probably have guessed, I personally prefer a written prayer; but I would never attempt to bind my opinion on anyone. So you be the judge! You decide!

The third point to be made is that the leading of public prayer is not as personal or detailed as private prayer, even though we may mention the sick and the bereaved by name in public prayer. With these exceptions, in public prayer we usually present the skeleton, a fill-in-the-blanks type of lead to enable the listeners to add personal and detailed facts in their prayer thoughts. For example, the leader might say, "Please, Lord, forgive us of our sins," while the listener may "fill in the blank" with: "Yes! Lord forgive me for losing my temper this morning!"

So you see there is a great deal of difference between private prayer (personal and detailed) and the leading of public prayer (general statements so the listener can fill in the blanks with personal and detailed thoughts).

Now that the stage has been set with these three points, let's turn our attention to the line-by-line use of the model prayer as an aid in leading public prayer.

<u>Our Father Who Art In Heaven</u>
Here again, we acknowledge that God is our father, and therefore that we should respect and obey Him. <u>Hallowed Be Thy Name.</u> Perhaps, in leading a public prayer we, at the beginning express more praise for God than in private prayer. The abundance of praise helps to center the worshipper's mind on God and to instill the proper respectful attitude for the remainder of the prayer. For example, the leader might say, "Almighty God, our heavenly father, we approach thy throne of grace with thanksgiving and humility. We are thankful, holy Father, for _____ (enumerate blessings). And we are humble Heavenly Father when we

realize that we have sinned and fallen short of the example set by your son and our Savior, Jesus.

NOTE:When praising God, be careful not to say anything that you don't believe or feel in your heart. God hates phonies and the audience will sense the falseness.

Thy Kingdom Grow; Thy Will Be Done

What are the things that will help the kingdom grow? What are the things that will promote love, peace, unity, and obedience on earth as it is in heaven? Included would be the following for which we should ask God's blessings:

- ❖ Preachers and teachers in presenting the gospel.
- ❖ Personal workers in leading others to Christ.
- ❖ Foreign missionaries in presenting the gospel.
- ❖ Skilled hands in helping the sick to recover.
- ❖ The various levels of government, guided by God's Word, in promoting freedom of worship and holiness in our nation.
- ❖ Our efforts to comfort the bereaved and the ultimate comfort that comes from Jesus.

Give Us This Day our Daily Bread

Here, again, we should thank the Lord for His past providence and pray that He will continue to provide us with the things which He sees that we are in need of. Then, too, this is a good time to pray that we share, with those in need, whatever the surplus the Lord has given to us (Luke 3:11).

Forgive Us Our Sins

At the beginning of our prayer we stated our humility because of our sin. Here we again acknowledge our sin by pointing out that we have done things that violated God's commands (sins of commission) and that we have left undone many things that we should have done (sins of omission, James 4:17). (At this time the listener should be thinking of personal and detailed instances in their own lives of sins of commission and omission. Together we all pray for forgiveness of our sins.)

Lead Us Not Into Temptation
Strengthen us, Lord so that we can overcome sin. Give us wisdom to find the way of escape when we are tempted. Strengthen us in our weakness that we may live more helpful, holy, lives.

For Thine is the Kingdom, Power, and the Glory
Help us Lord to give Thee all the praise and to depend upon Thy grace and goodness.

In Christ Name we pray. Amen.
Have you learned anything about your new relationship to prayer? Test your knowledge by working the exercises "Let's See What You've Learned" and "Now, Let's Get Personal."

Section II: Let's See What You've Learned
1. What advantages are offered by prayer?

_____

_____

_____

2. What is prayer? _____

_____

_____

3. When is the right time for prayer?

_____

_____

4. What does it mean: "Pray without ceasing"?

_____

_____

_____

5. What circumstances can "kill" our prayerful mood?

_____

_____

6. What is the right position for prayer?

_____

_____

7. What is the right attitude for prayer?

_____

_____

_____

8. What is the right address for prayer?

_____

_____

9. Why must we pray with importunity?

_____

_____

_____

10. Why cannot the model prayer rightfully be called "the Lord's Prayer? _____

    _____

    _____

11. What pledge is inferred when we address God as "our Father who art in heaven?" _____

    _____

    _____

    _____

12. If we constantly take the Lord's name in vain what line of the model prayer in particular should we NOT pray?

    _____

    _____

13. Why should the line of the Model Prayer "Thy Kingdome Come" be changed to "Thy Kingdom grow" in the Christian era? _____

    _____

    _____

14. Why is the line of the model prayer "Thy Will Be Done on Earth" considered to be a challenge to every Christian? _____

    _____

    _____

15. Should a person pray for luxuries? Explain.

_____

_____

_____

16. What two things will prevent a Christian's sins from being forgiven? _____

_____

_____

17. When a brother has sinned against us, why should we forgive him even if he fails to apologize?

_____

_____

_____

_____

18. In question 17 (above) what else should we do?

_____

_____

_____

19. The line of the model prayer "Lead Us Not Into Temptation" is really asking God to do what?

_____

_____

_____

20. In what two ways does God deliver us from evil?

_____

_____

_____

_____

21. What is the major difference between private prayer and the leading of public prayer?

_____

_____

_____

22. What does the word "amen" mean?

_____

_____

_____

23. What advantages are gained from a written prayer?

_____

_____

_____

24. Why is leading public prayer difficult?

_____

_____

_____

25. When the leader prays, "Please help the sick to get well." What should each member of the listeners respond in their prayer thoughts? _____

_____

_____

26. What precautions should a person take while leading a public prayer and praising God? _____

_____

_____

_____

27. For what four types of people should we pray in asking aid to those in spreading the gospel? _____

_____

_____

_____

28. What prayer should we pray where doctors and nurses are concerned? _____

_____

_____

29. What prayer should we pray for our government?

_____

_____

_____

30. How should the bereaved be comforted?

_____

_____

_____

Section III: Now Let's Get Personal

1. How do you think your prayer life can be improved?

_____

_____

_____

2. During the day, what circumstances that you normally encounter take you completely out of prayerful mood?

_____

_____

_____

3. What changes can you make to insure that you will keep your prayerful mood? _____

_____

_____

4. What Christian acts do you keep postponing? What causes you to delay? And how can you overcome your lack of motivation? _____

_____

_____

_____

5. Do you ever practice leading a prayer at home? Do you think this would help you in leading public prayer? What effect does this practice have on you? On other people at home? _____

_____

_____

6. Verses to Memorize:

    Matthew 6:9-13

    I Thessalonians 5:17

    Ecclesiastes 2:13

    James 1:6

    James 4:3

    Matthew 6:15

    Luke   3:11

Chapter XI. YOUR NEW RELATIONSHIP WITH THE LORD'S SUPPER

Section 1: Let's Talk About It.

Have you ever played a role in a play? If so you will probably remember that you had a dress rehearsal before you gave a public performance. This was a wise thing to do.

And Jesus, in Hs wisdom, also had a dress rehearsal for the observance of the "Lord's supper." On the Thursday night before Hs crucifixion, the Lord and Hs disciples were in the upper room celebrating the Passover. On that occasion, as recorded in Matthew 26:26-28:

> "...Jesus took bread blessed it, broke
> it, and gave it to the disciples, and said, Take
> eat; this is my body. And he took the cup
> and gave thanks, and gave it to them, saying,
> Drink ye all of it; for this is my blood of the
> New Testament which is shed for many for
> the remission of sins."

Thus, He did teach His disciples how to hold a memorial service for Him after his death.

The Lord's Supper is a time of communion with Jesus and His sacrifice. It has certain characteristics, and it should be observed with several precautions. Let's first discuss the characteristics of the Lord's Supper.

CHARACTERISTICS OF THE LORD'S SUPPER

The Lord's Supper actually has each of the Following characteristics:
- ❖ A funeral service.
- ❖ A time to express gratitude.
- ❖ A period of self-examination.
- ❖ A victory celebration.

❖ A prophecy of the future.

The Lord's Supper is a Funeral Service

In I Corinthians 11:26 we are told that during the Lord's Supper we should show the Lord's death till He comes again. This means that it is a permanent memorial to be observed until Jesus comes again. And by inspired example we are told to observe it on the first day of the week (Acts 20:7).

But remember it is a funeral service and should be conducted in a quiet and dignified manner, with sadness for the suffering and death of our Lord. This is definitely not a time for conversation with friends, nor any other form of disrespect. If a funeral was being held for your best friend, how would you feel and act? Well, Jesus is our best friend and He gave His life for us; so always act respectfully.

At a funeral service for our best friend, we would, no doubt, want to view the body. It is true that we cannot view the actual body of Jesus because He is no longer with us. But in our mind's eyes we can see the bruised and bloody back of our friend Jesus, see the blood running from the crown of thorns, see the painful piercing of His hands and feet by cruel nails, and finally see His pierced side as He hung suspended on the cross.

Then, in our mind's eye we shift our gaze to the sealed tomb where our Lord lay in his death shroud. And we wonder at the great love that lead Him to take our place on the cross and in the tomb.

The Lord's Supper Is a Time To Express Gratitude

How grateful we should be that the Lord took our place during His suffering before the cross, during His pain on the cross, and during His death. Before the cross, Christ was beaten with a Roman whip, having several throngs, each with sharp pieces of metal, designed to rip a back to shreds. For our sins, we—not Jesus—deserved the beating. And how His scalp and forehead must have been torn by the crown of thorns that He wore in our place. Then, how He suffered as the spikes were driven through His hands and feet and the cross jolted hard into the ground, tearing His nailed flesh. For our sins, we deserved that punishment, but Jesus took our place. How grateful we should be as we tearfully remember the pain Jesus bore for you and for me. Were we worth all of His suffering? The answer is "No!" But our Lord was gracious enough to endure it for our sake.

The Lord's Supper Is A Period for Self-Examination

I Corinthians 11:28 tells us to examine ourselves, to test ourselves, to compare ourselves to the standard set by Jesus Christ. Do we have the self-control of Jesus that led Him to remain on the cross even though He could have asked God to remove Him? Do we have the mercy shown by Jesus when He prayed for forgiveness for those who murdered and tormented Him? And do we have the kindness that Jesus showed as He went about doing good in both action and words? To each of these questions, I can only answer: "No!" I fall far short of Jesus' self-control, forgiveness, and kindness; and I pray that the Lord will help me to grow toward the standard set by Jesus. Won't you join me in the prayer for me and for you?

The Lord's Supper Is A Victory Celebration

Can Christ's crucifixion really be a victory? Yes! In two ways it can. Christ was victorious over Satan, and He was victorious over death.

The Victory over Satan

Satan had the whole world trapped within his grasp. Only a perfect sacrifice could redeem mankind by satisfying divine justice. But no perfect sacrifice was available because all men had sinned (Romans 3:23). Then God came out with a perfect plan: send sinless Jesus to die for our sins and thus make possible our rescue from the Devil's grasp. How Satan must have shuddered at the brilliance of the plan. What was Satan to do in order to preserve his grasp on mankind? He had it! Satan would get Jesus to "sell out" by offering several enticing rewards: turn stones into bread to ease a 40-day hunger, have Jesus jump from a high building to gain fame and popularity; and have Jesus bow to Satan in order to gain the rule of all the kingdom of the world. But Jesus still did not give up His mission of salvation.

Day by day, then, Satan tempted Jesus in every way that you and I are tempted (Hebrews 4:15), and Jesus still did not weaken.

Finally, with Jesus on the cross, Satan tried his strongest temptation: "Jesus, call for 6,000 angels to take you down from the cross and kill all these murderers and tormentors!' But Jesus was faithful to His mission: He not only remained faithful to the death on the cross, but He also prayed for the forgiveness of His enemies. Jesus could not be swayed from obeying God. He remained true till death. Jesus won the victory; Satan was defeated.

The Victory over Death

When Jesus arose from the grave, He had conquered death; and His victory made it possible for us to arise victorious over death, if we remain as faithful to God as Jesus did. In what form will we arise? I don't know, but I do know we will have a new body that is superior to the old one. It will be a glorious body, less apt to break down or wear out. No doctor or hospital bills in heaven! But that's looking into the future.

The Lord's Supper Is a Prophecy

In I Corinthians 11:26, we are told that we should observe the Lord's supper until he comes again. This is a clear prophecy of His second coming. When will this second coming occur? No one knows for certain, but we know for certain that Christ will come again some day. When Jesus was asked by His disciples when the world would end, He said that only the Heavenly Father knew (Matthew 24:35, 36). He said that neither He nor angels knew the answer. Jesus also pointed out that the Lord's coming would be like a thief in the night, at a time when no one was expecting Him (Matthew 24:42-44). Then those who predict that the Lord will come on a certain date should be more careful: Do they really know more than Jesus and the angels?

PRECAUTIONS ABOUT OBSERVING THE LORD'S SUPPER

We can never be worthy of the sacrifice made by our Lord, but we can partake of the Lord's Supper in a worthily manner. To partake in an unworthily manner is to eat and drink damnation to our souls (I Corinthians 11:29). But what is a worthily manner?

Since partaking of the Lord's Supper is an act of worship, we must partake in spirit and truth (John 4:23). To partake in spirit means that our hearts are in the observance of the Lord's Supper. To partake in truth means we are partaking in a manner that the Bible describes as proper.

Partaking in Spirit

If we partake of the Lord's Supper while our thoughts are on next month's car payment, the insult we received yesterday, or the baby crying in row six, we have sinned. We have not kept our heart set on the loving sacrifice of Christ. But how can we prevent the crying baby or the talking pair behind us from taking our minds off the funeral service of our Lord? Sometimes it's hard to concentrate and we need some kind of device to help us. You can probably think of an aid for concentrating on the Lord's Supper. In case you cannot perhaps you could use mine: I cross my ankles about where Christ's ankles were nailed to the cross and I try to visualize His pain. I also dig my right thumb strongly into my left palm to produce a mild pain to help me concentrate. And in my mind's eye, I go step-by-step through the mistreatment and suffering of our dear Lord. It does seem to help me keep in mind the memorial for our Lord.

Partaking In Truth
While attending church services conducted in a Philippine dialect, I sang the songs in English while the congregation sang in the dialect. Everything went well except I was singing verse 4 while they were singing verse 3, and some of the Filipinos understood English. They did seem puzzled.

But next, it was my turn to be puzzled when I heard them speak of "apple-juice." "What?" I thought, have they substituted apple juice for grape juice in the Lord's Supper?" After the service, I challenged the preacher and then found out they were saying "Apos Dios" meaning "sir God" which sounded just like "apple-juice.'

Which brings me to the point: we should not try to substitute anything, say buttermilk and cornbread, for grape-juice and unleavened bread in the Lord's Supper. And neither should we substitute any of our think-so in observing the Lord's Supper.

The Lord's Supper remember, is a funeral, and we should not employ cheering for the Lord, turning flips, or screaming, "We love you." Since this is a funeral, we should do everything decently and in order (I Corinthians 14:40).

And the ushers passing out the grape juice and crackers to the audience should be as silent and unnoticed as possible to prevent distracting the worshipper. They are performing an important task which can help or hinder those observing the Lord's Supper. Lord, help us always be a help to the worshippers by our quiet and efficient service.

How much have you learned? Check to see the answer by working "Section II. Let's See What You've Learned" and "Section III. Now Let's Get Personal"

Section II: Let's See What You've Learned

1. When did Jesus perform a "dress rehearsal" of the Lord's Supper? _____

_____

2. Why is the Lord's Supper correctly called a funeral service? _____

_____

_____

3. During the observance of the Lord's Supper, why should we be grateful? _____

_____

_____

4. What is meant by the statement that the Lord's Supper is a time for self-examination? _____

_____

_____

_____

5. For what two reasons is the Lord's Supper a Victory
   celebration? _____

   _____

   _____

   _____

6. Why do we say that the Lord's Supper is also a time of
   prophecy? _____

   _____

   _____

7. When will the world end? _____

   _____

   _____

   _____

8. What is the significance of Jesus resurrection?

   _____

   _____

   _____

9. What serious warning does the Bible give about
   partaking of the Lord's Supper? _____

   _____

   _____

   _____

10. How can we partake of the Lord's Supper in an unworthy manner? _____

_____

_____

_____

Section III: Now Let's Get Personal

1. Does your mind drift into unrelated matters during the Lord's Supper? _____

_____

_____

2. If so, how do you plan to improve your observance of the memorial? _____

_____

_____

3. Do people around you talk during the Lord's supper? What should be your reaction to them?

_____

_____

_____

4. In your mind's eye do you see the blood and broken body of our Lord during the memorial service? _____ How do you plan to sharpen this

mental image in your minds' eye? _____

_____

_____

5. While performing self-examination related to the Lord's supper, what areas, if any, do you see in which you need to improve? _____

_____

6. How do you plan to make the needed improvements, if any? _____

_____

_____

Chapter XII. YOUR NEW RELATIONSHIP WITH CROSS BEARING

Section 1: Let's Talk About It.

Will you and I react the same to similar circumstances? Not necessarily! People often react differently. For example, I am thinking of two men who faced torture, shame and ridicule. One of the men – Samson – hated his tormentors and attempted to destroy them. The other man – Jesus – loved His tormentors and prayed for their forgiveness. Samson carried his "cross" with hatred and Jesus carried His cross with love. If you had a cross to bear, what would be your attitude?

Will you and I ever have a "cross" to bear? Yes! Definitely yes! Anyone who will live a godly life in Christ Jesus will suffer persecution (II Timothy 3:12), and that is a promise of God just as much as salvation of the obedient believer is a promise.

Can you and I escape bearing our cross? Yes! There is a way, but the cost is too much to pay! Our souls! But there was a way that a young Christian discovered. He went into army camp where the men were not noted for the purity of their lives nor their language. And they did love to fight – off base. When the young Christian returned on furlough, he was asked by a friend, "How did you get along in that rough army camp?" "Oh," the young man answered, "I had no problem at all; I was careful to keep the men from finding out that I was a Christian." That's one way to avoid punishment in this world all right, but what about punishment in the world to come?

As Christians we are often called upon to oppose evil circumstances and to stand up for Christ. The embarrassment and ridicule we may receive are just splinters from the cross we bear. They gouge into our spiritual flesh and pain us, but they are a necessary part of cross bearing.

But a faithful Christian must bear a cross. One song we sing asks us the question: "Must Jesus Bear the Cross Alone?" And in that same song, the answer comes ringing back: "No, there's a cross for everyone and there's a cross for me." To be a Christian, a faithful follower of Christ, we cannot escape bearing a cross.

This being so, cross bearing is a subject worthy of our detailed discussion. In this discussion, we cover the symbolic meaning of the cross, the pain of the cross, what it means to shoulder our cross, and the Christian growth that results from our cross bearing.

THE MEANING OF THE CROSS

Originally, the word "cross" meant a sharp-pointed stake on which the Syrians impaled serious offenders. Later, the Romans introduced the Latin cross, a vertical pole with a short crossbar. But regardless of its shape, the cross symbolized great shame and was usually cruel.

The Shame of the Cross
The cross was not normally used as a method of capital punishment by the Jews, who preferred to stone serious offenders to death for such crimes as blasphemy, cursing a parent, murder, homosexuality and adultery. However, after the offender had been killed, the Jews hung the dead body on a tree to show the shame of the person and his family. And it was said, "Cursed is everyone that hangeth on a tree."

But under Roman rule, the Jews could not (legally) execute a person without Roman approval; and the Roman courts preferred crucifixion as a means of capital punishment. But even then, this method of execution was beset with shame, greatly increased by hostile crowds who tormented the one suffering execution—and suffering is a good word because this method of execution was filled with severe pain experienced over a long period of time.

The Pain of the Cross
Have you ever stepped on a nail? How did it feel? Not very pleasant! In fact it plain hurt! But now suppose what the nail was still in your foot, some person (certainly not a friend) kept the nail in your foot while he moved it back and forth and round and round. Oh! What pain! But that is mild compared with what Jesus felt in being placed on the cross. These nails were bigger, almost as big as railroad spikes. And how they tore the flesh with agonizing pain when the cross was jolted into the ground. At last the pain was over! Not so! Far from it! The pain had just begun.

To breathe a person on the cross had to raise himself up high to get a breath of air – what did this do to the pain on the hands and feet? Then, as he grew tired he had to sag down again – another jolt of hard pain in both hands and feet. And this could continue for many hours.

But then came another type of pain – spiritual pain. The people whom Jesus had befriended stood around mocking him: "Come down from the cross if you can." While the spiritual leaders of the Jews joined in the cat-calls: "he saved others; himself he cannot save. Come down from the cross and we will believe you." All this was severe spiritual pain, but the worst was yet to come: the feeling of guilt that Jesus felt for all the sins of the world; past, present, and future. When you have sinned do you remember the throb and ache of your guilty conscience? Now multiply that feeling by one billion people and the hundreds of sins each one had committed and you have an idea of the severity of guilt that Jesus felt. And you know why God could not bear to see His pure son bearing such a terrible load of guilt, so He turned His face away. And at that moment feeling the terrible loneliness without His father, Jesus called out in deepest spiritual anguish, "My God, My God! Why hast Thou forsaken me?"

Such pain as that you and I will never have to bear, unless we are condemned to hell where we too will cry from the flames, "My God, My God! Why hast Thou forsaken me?" But there is one essential difference. If we are there we will deserve it and we will know why we are there: And that knowledge, my friend, would make the punishment even worse. We must either bear our cross here or bear the flames hereafter. (Knowing the terror of the Lord, we persuade men II Corinthians 5:11).

SHOULDERING OUR CROSS

In Matthew 16:24, Jesus is recorded as saying:
"…If any man will come after me, let him deny himself and take up his cross and follow me."

Let's examine this verse by first asking a question: "Where is Jesus now?" "In heaven seated at the right hand of God," you say? Correct. (Romans 8:34) Good answer! Do you or do you not wish to follow Him? The alternative looks pretty dismal, does it not? Yes, we all hope to follow Jesus to heaven. Then Jesus gives us the correct map that points out our way to heaven and on it we see such landmarks as the following:

- ❖ Deny yourself.
- ❖ Take up your cross.
- ❖ Follow Jesus
- ❖ Now, let's add a question: How often?

Let's discuss each of these landmarks on the way to heaven.

Deny yourself

Deny yourself what? A new car? A new dress? A new boat for the lake? The daily candy and Coke that

makes us fat? Attend a movie instead of reading the Bible?
Yes! These are some of the things that a Christian might
decide to do without. These might help the church
contribution too, and are commendable. But this is NOT
what it means to deny yourself.

To deny yourself means to deny that you as a
person even exist, or as the Apostle Paul has said, "I live,
yet not I but Christ liveth in me" (Galatians 2:20). And he
also said, "For me to live is Christ" (Philippians 1:21).
What Paul is actually saying is that he tests his every
thought, word, or action to see if the Lord would approve
of them before he uses the. In other words, Paul tries to
think with the mind of Christ. But how can a person think
with another person's mind? Can it be done? Yes! To
explain: Farmer Jones carefully taught his son all about
farming. The son saw his every action and listened to his
every word. Then Farmer Jones died, leaving his teenage
son to care for the family farm. Whenever any problem
came along, his son would ask himself this question:
"What would Pa have done under these circumstances?"
And what would help him think thus, "to think with the
mind of Pa?" Remembering what Pa has said and done.

Wouldn't it be wonderful to be able to think with
the mind of Christ? Yes, Indeed! But we do have the mind
of Christ (I Corinthians 2:16). Where do we have it? In the
Bible which shows the word and actions of the Lord Jesus.
By studying the Bible carefully we can eventually learn to
think like the Lord Jesus – to have His mind. When this
has been done, we can truly say, "We have denied
ourselves" because we are thinking, not like our old self,
but with the mind of Christ, which will help us decide
really to pick up our cross.

Taking Up Our Cross
Which of our crosses is the heaviest – yours or
mine? And are they exactly the same or different? No two

people have the same cross to bear because each of us has different abilities and different opportunities. Now, here's a spiritual mathematical formula for you to memorize.

ABILITY + OPPORTUNITY = RESPONSIBILTY

God does not hold us responsible for doing thing if He has not blessed us with the required ability (Luke 12:48). And God does not hold us responsible for taking advantage of opportunities that we are not aware of. But when we know of the opportunity and have the ability to do a good work and fail to do it, we have sinned (James 4:17).

Why do I bring this up in a discussion of cross bearing? For one reason, a part of cross bearing is to do what Jesus needs us to do rather than what we want to do at any given time, providing we have the ability. This may be painful in anticipation (a splinter from the cross); but after you sacrifice your own interest to do the Lord's work, you will find that the pain is deadened by the anesthesia of Christian joy.

And here's another reason for presenting our spiritual mathematical formula in this chapter. The more abilities you have and the more your talents are needed and used, the less time you have to fulfill personal wishes. Not only that, but your successes in using your talents may lead some of your friends to envy you and may require your patience and your pain (More splinters from the cross).

And besides the spiritual mathematical formula, the other splinters such as the following may pierce you in your cross bearing:

❖ When you remember to thank the Lord for your food at a café. Others may classify you as a fanatic. Is the giving of thanks a Christian thing to do? Then do it!

❖ When you day, "If the Lord wills, I'll see you tomorrow." They may give you a funny look and think you are a "goody two shoes," but you have been humble and have witnessed for the Lord (Never mind the splinters).

❖ When you refuse to tell or listen to dirty jokes or to take the Lord's name in vain, they may sneer at you now, but later they will respect you.

❖ When you refuse to bow to peer pressure, to engage in drugs, to drink alcoholic beverages, or to smoke tobacco, they may call you a square (or a cube), but whose brain will be cooked, whose liver damaged, and whose lungs will have cancer? But more important, your actions have pleased the Lord, which you should do rather than to try to please man (Acts 5:29).

❖ When a person has insulted you, bite your tongue and give a soft answer rather than strike back verbally and cause a scene which would destroy your Christian influence (That bite on your tongue is another splinter from your cross).

❖ Refuse to gossip – and oh, at times this is difficult – when a person has spoken shabbily to you or treated you badly. Instead, go talk gently with the person and settle your differences.

❖ Insist on going to Bible class and church even though an invitation from a friend to do otherwise seems so appealing (This is a BIG splinter).

❖ Continue your daily Bible study even though some of your favorite TV programs may be on (This takes real determination – how much determination led Jesus to the cross?).

❖ Do whatever good deeds you can do to help the church and individual church members even if you must skip some of your favorite activities (Happiness comes from the things we can do without in order to help others – Acts 20:35).

This is not a complete list of suggestions for bearing your cross. With the experience of living and with more Bible study you probably can supplement the list.

But why bother? What good does it do you to make all these sacrifices and to suffer all the splinters of bearing your cross? Is it really worthwhile? Yes! If we intend to devote our lives to following Jesus.

Following Jesus

In discussing the following of Jesus, we need to consider three questions: How close, how far, and how often?

How Close

How close should we follow Jesus? What things would prevent us from being close to him? We must be careful that other people and the lies of Satan do not separate us from Jesus. Satan is glad to tell us such lies as the following:

❖ Just this once won't hurt anything.
❖ But everybody is doing it.
❖ This is a little different from outright sinning.
❖ Because of what they did to me I have a right to _____.
❖ I'm not taking vengeance; I'm just getting even.
❖ I can quit anytime I want to.
❖ I'm doing evil that good may come of it.
❖ Since it is my birthday, it won't be a sin.
❖ Because we love each other, it will be all right (Sponsored by Hollywood).

❖ Other lame reasons and excuses you have heard other people use to justify sinning.

We should be careful not to let other people's selfish desires or false reasons separate us from the loving and forgiving side of Jesus – and we should follow him closely no matter how far we must go.

How Far With Jesus

We sometimes sing the song "Oh to be Like Thee," which is a prayer. Do we really want to be like Jesus: to think what He would think, to say what He would say and to do what He would do? In other word, do we want to <u>follow the example</u> of Jesus? The Apostle Peter says that we should follow Jesus example (I Peter 2:21). I'm sure that we Christians all have a desire to follow Jesus. After all, that's what the word "Christian" means: A follower of Jesus. The question is not will we follow Jesus – which any of us would probably do if it is comfortable or convenient – but rather the question is, will we follow Him under uncomfortable and inconvenient circumstances? In other words, how far will we go in following Jesus?

How far will you follow Jesus? Will you follow Jesus into the water of baptism, as recorded in Matthew 3:16? Will you follow Him that far? Most of you have already done so. Congratulations on following Jesus that far.

How far will you follow Jesus? Will you follow Him in resisting temptations like He did as recorded in Matthew 4:1-11? Lord grant you strength to do so. Will you follow Him that far?

How far will you follow Jesus? Will you follow Him in proclaiming the kingdom and telling others of God's love? Have you told your friends and neighbors about Jesus and His message? Will you follow Him that far?

How far will you follow Jesus? Will you follow Him in going about helping other people: in feeding the hungry, in giving drink to the thirsty, in visiting the sick, in welcoming strangers, in praying for the benefit of other people, and in visiting those in jail? Will you follow Him that far?

How far will you follow Jesus? Will you follow Him in His trial where He was ridiculed and humiliated? Or at the slightest hint of criticism will you stop working for the Lord? Will you follow Jesus that far?

How far will you follow Jesus? Will you follow Him and remain faithful in spite of scourging, that is, the chastisement that comes from the Lord (Hebrews 12:4-7)? Will you follow Him that far?

How far will you follow Jesus? Will you follow Him as He stumbled beneath the weight of the cross? Will you pray for strength to carry on when your tasks as a Christian seem too heavy, to overwhelm you? Will you follow Him that far?

How far will you follow Jesus? Will you follow Him all the way to the cross? As Jesus laid down His life for us, will you lay down the living of your life for the sake of other people? Will you follow Him that far?

Lord, help us to keep shouldering our cross and to learn to follow Jesus all the way – all the way my Savior leads me. If we do so, there is great reward.

THE GROWTH THAT COMES FROM CROSS BEARING

What growth comes from cross bearing? While bearing a cross we grow in the same four ways that Jesus grew as a teenager, in wisdom, in stature, and in favor with God and man (Luke 2:52). However, in our discussion of these four items, we will give some reservations as you will later see.

Growth in Wisdom

When does a person actually start to develop wisdom? Can we pinpoint a definite age to show the beginning of wisdom? No! Some people develop wisdom early in life while others live a lifetime without developing it. Instead of asking when does wisdom develop, perhaps a better question would be: "What is wisdom? There are two types of wisdom described in the Bible: A devilish, or worldly type of wisdom described in James 3:14-16. You can read about it if you chose; but it's a type we do NOT want to develop. The other type of wisdom is the good type and is described as follows in James 3:17,18:

❖ Pure
❖ Peaceable
❖ Gentle
❖ Easy to be entreated
❖ Full of mercy
❖ Full of good fruits
❖ Without partiality
❖ Without hypocrisy

How does cross bearing help to develop this kind of wisdom? In cross bearing, we are not seeking to please ourselves but are seeking to serve others. Since our minds are not clouded with envy, hate, and unselfish thoughts, we can think more reasonable – wiser. This also keeps us from being seen as "small" in other people's eyes.

Growth in Stature

Luke 2:52 refers to Jesus' growth in physical size. Here, let's use it to refer to growth in spiritual size, growth in the use of our talents, growth in knowledge of the Bible, and growth in Christian good works. Growth in all of these areas are produced by our bearing of the cross.

Growth in Favor with God

Whom does God favor more than Jesus? "No one," you say? And you are right. So the more we resemble Jesus in thought, word, and deed, the more we will be favored by God. As you grow more and more like Jesus you are more and more in favor with God. You might remember a little poem (given to me by my seventh grade teacher). It goes this way:

> Good, better,
> best;
> Never let it
> rest
> Till your good
> is better
> And your
> better, best.

Good advice for one wanting to imitate Christ.

Growth in Favor With Man

Will bearing a cross make you popular with all people? Christ warns us about giving what is holy to the dogs or casting your pearls before swine that may turn and bite you. Not all people will appreciate your Christian living because it may make them feel guilty. But most Christians and the ones you serve will appreciate your good works. But more important, Christ will appreciate them.

That completes our discussion of cross bearing. To see what you have learned, work "Section II. Let's See What You've Learned" and "Section III. Let's Get Personal."

P.S. If you have made a wholehearted effort throughout this course of study, I believe that your Christian growth will probably surpass many who have been Christians much longer than you. If so, don't be lifted up with pride. Remember that it was only with the help of

God that you have come this far. Be wise—remember who has given you the victory, as pointed out in the poem, "Keep Me Wise," found in the appendix at the back of the book.

After reading that poem, then proceed with your working of Section II and Section III of this chapter and God Speed to you!

Section II: Let's See What You've Learned

1. Why do different people vary in their reaction to persecution? _____

_____

_____

2. What is the only way you or I can escape bearing a cross? _____

_____

_____

3. What is the symbolic meaning of the cross in Christ's life? _____

_____

_____

4. And today? _____

_____

_____

_____

5. What types of pain did Jesus experience on the cross?

_____

_____

_____

_____

6. While on the cross, why did Jesus groan: "My God! My God! Why hast thou forsaken me?"_____

_____

_____

_____

7. What things must we do before we can follow Jesus?

_____

_____

_____

8. What does it mean "to deny yourself?"

_____

_____

_____

_____

9. How can a person learn to think with the mind of Christ? _____

_____

_____

_____

10. What is the spiritual mathematic formula for responsibility? _____

_____

_____

11. What deadens the pain of self-denial if we are Christian? _____

_____

_____

12. Why does a many-talented man suffer more than a single-talented man? _____

_____

_____

13. While bearing a cross, what are some of the things which may cause you to sin? _____

_____

_____

14. What are some of the excuses Satan will give you to help separate you from Jesus? _____

_____

_____

_____

15. What growth results from cross bearing?

_____

_____

_____

_____

16. What are the characteristics of the wisdom that comes
from cross bearing? _____

_____

_____

_____

17. Why does cross bearing help us grow in favor with
God? _____

_____

_____

_____

Explain: Some people will and some people will not
appreciate our cross bearing.

_____

_____

_____

_____

_____

_____

Section III: Now Let's Get Personal

1. What is the biggest cross you have to bear?

_____

George J. Cunningham, Sr.

_____

_____

2. How do you make it lighter? _____

_____

_____

_____

_____

3. What kind of spiritual pain has cross bearing brought to you? _____

_____

_____

4. What are you now doing in order to learn how to deny yourself? _____

_____

_____

_____

5. What additional things can you help to speed up your learning to deny yourself? _____

_____

_____

_____

6. What talents do you possess that you are not yet using for the Lord? _____

_____

_____

_____

7. How do you plan to use these talents?

_____

_____

_____

8. Rate yourself either yes or no in the blanks before each of the following items:

_____ Do you refuse to thank God at a café for a meal?

_____ Do you forget to say; "If the Lord Wills" before telling someone you will see them tomorrow?

_____ Do you bow to peer pressure in doing things you know are wrong?

_____ When someone insults you do you strike back?

_____ Do you gossip?

_____ Do you skip Bible Class for other forms of activity?

_____ Do you allow TV to interrupt your Bible study?

For each "yes" answer, tell how you plan to overcome this type of action or lack of action.

_____

_____

_____

_____

_____

_____

9. In the space before each item listed place a "yes" if you comply with the characteristic and a "no" if you do not.

_____Pure

_____Peaceable

_____Gentle

_____Easy to be entreated

_____Full of mercy

_____Full of good fruits

_____Without partiality

_____Without hypocrisy

In the spaces below, tell how you will develop each of the Characteristic for which you answered "no".

_____

_____

_____

_____

_____

Chapter XIII. YOUR NEW RELATIONSHIP WITH THE CHRISTIAN GRACES

Section 1: Let's Talk About It.

Have you ever watched a can being crushed by a vacuum? Not really! Technically speaking, the vacuum only allowed the air pressure outside the can to crush the can. "Nature hates a vacuum" and will rapidly seek to fill it with something.

This is equally true in the spiritual realm: Nature will attempt to fill emptiness with something - - either good or evil. Do we have a clear teaching about this fact in the Bible? Yes! Let's look closely at Matthew 12:43-45 which, in effect contains a stern warning:

> "When the unclean spirit is gone out of a
> man, he [the unclean spirit] walketh through
> dry places, seeking rest, and findeth none.
> The he [the unclean spirit] saith, I will return
> into my house from whence I came out; and
> when he is come, he findeth it empty, swept,
> and garnished. Then goeth he and taketh
> with himself seven other spirits more wicked
> than himself and they enter in and dwell
> there: And the last state of that man is
> worse than the first. Even so it be also unto
> this wicked generation." [Bracketed words
> are mine, needed for explanation].

Let's notice several things about this passage of scripture. First, notice that the man had been cleansed of his evil spirit just as we were during baptism. Notice, too, that the unclean spirit wanted to return, just as our old sins before baptism will try to return to our lives. But we will have Jesus' help in resisting them. Then, too, notice that if the old sins do manage to return, that they will bring other sins with them, because our yielding to sin makes it harder for us to seek the help of Christ. And finally, notice that we would be in worse condition than we were before baptism.

But let's not overlook the <u>key word</u> of this entire passage: the word <u>"empty."</u> If we don't fill our lives with something good after baptism, this wicked generation, working for Satan, will gladly fill our lives full of evil. But how can we prevent this from happening? To do so, we must fill our lives full of such good things as Bible study, church attendance and good deeds, all of which not only help to crowd out evil but also help us grow and Christians.

One way we must grow is in the Christian Graces. Growing in these graces will help us to be partakers of the nature of God (II Peter 1:4), will help us to be productive Christians, will help us to see more clearly, and will help to prevent our falling from our saved condition. -- Provided these graces are in us and abound (II Peter 1:8-10).

But what are these Christian graces? In II Peter 1:5-7 we find that they include:
- ❖ Faith
- ❖ Virtue
- ❖ Knowledge
- ❖ Temperance
- ❖ Patience
- ❖ Godliness
- ❖ Brotherly kindness
- ❖ Charity

Since our salvation may depend, among other things, on our growth in these graces, we should discuss them rather thoroughly: What they are and how to make them abound (be plentiful, grow).

Before discussing each of these graces, however, let me point out some general facts that apply to the graces as the whole. First, each of these graces probably exists to some degree in us before we start to grow as in the first one listed, faith. That is, we probably have some <u>Bible</u>

knowledge before we develop a full saving faith. A similar statement could be made about each of the Christian graces.

Another general fact is that we do not develop evenly in all of the graces. A person, for example, could be strong in <u>Bible</u> knowledge and weak in patience. But the main thing to remember is that we as Christians must grow in each of these graces to the full extent of our abilities, our efforts, and Jesus help will allow. By doing so, we will keep our lives so full of good things that Satan's influence will be crowded out, or at least greatly curbed.

Now, let's turn our attention to the first Christian grace to be discussed, that of faith.

FAITH

In discussing faith, we should cover the types of faith, a definition of faith, the necessity of having faith, and methods to use to make faith grow.

<u>The Types of Faith</u>
We are told that there <u>is only one faith </u>(Ephesians 4:5) and that we should contend earnestly for it (Jude 3). When used in this sense, faith refers to the <u>Bible,</u> the gospel, which we are forbidden to change according to the Apostle Paul (Galatians 1:8,9) and the Apostle John (Revelations 22:18,19).

But faith is used in another sense in the Bible. It is used to refer to the personal faith of a believer which is sometimes described as little (Matthew 6:30), great (Matthew 8:10), weak (Romans 14:1), strong (Romans 4:20), working (Galatians 5:6), and dead (James 2:20). When used in this personal sense, faith should change and should grow. It is in this second sense that we will cover faith in the rest of this discussion.

A Definition of Faith

Let's begin by telling what faith is NOT. Faith does not consist of things which can be perceived by human senses. We Christians should walk by faith and <u>not</u> by sight (II Corinthians 5:7). Will we have faith that heaven exists after we actually enter heaven? No! Faith will have been swallowed up by sight, by reality. So in describing faith, remember that we are talking about unseen things and about our hope for the future.

In Hebrews 11:1, we are told that faith is:

❖ The substance of things hoped for.
❖ The evidence of things not seen.

What is the substance of our faith? It is our <u>firm conviction</u> that heaven exists and that it will someday be a place occupied by faithful believers. What is the evidence of things not seen? The evidence is the <u>handiwork</u> of God (Psalms 19:1; Romans 1:20), the earth in all its glory, that declare that God exists and that he is the all-powerful, all-wise, and all-loving creator.

But before we leave our discussion of faith, however, let's clear up an additional point: Faith means more than mental assent that God exists. After all, the devils believe and tremble (James 2:19). Do they have a saving faith? To see the true meaning of faith, let's compare the teachings of two Bible verses: John 3:16 says that a person who <u>believes</u> in Jesus will be saved; while Hebrews 5:9 says that Jesus saves those who obey him. Is this a contradiction? No! The two verses merely explain and reinforce each other. When we combine their meanings we see that a saving faith is one where the belief is strong enough to lead a person to obey Jesus. Romans 16:26 refers to faith in this sense also as it talks about the "<u>obedience of faith</u>."

But is such faith necessary? Is it important? Why should we develop such a faith?

The Importance of Faith

If I promised to give you $50 if you would walk one mile to my house, assuming I was sincere, what would determine whether or not you received the $50? Two things: Whether or not you believed that the $50 existed and whether or not you diligently sought for it – walked to my house.

Next let's read Hebrews 11:6. By doing so, you will see that to please God we must do two things:

❖ Believe that He exists (Faith).
❖ Believe He is a rewarder of those who diligently seek Him.

We have already discussed what it means to believe that God exists in our definition of faith. We also pointed out that the faith we were talking about requires obedience. Do you suppose that obedience could be said to mean "diligently seeking God?" After all, we are told that our sins (disobedience to God) would separate us from God (Isaiah 59:2); then it would seem to follow that obedience would lead us closer to God…diligently seeking him. Think about it!

So is faith in God important? Yes! As is diligently seeking God? We must have a faith that causes us to seek God in order to be pleasing to him. Is our faith in God that strong? If not, we should desire that our faith should grow. And even if our faith is already strong, it still may need to grow even stronger.

How to Make Faith Grow

In a nutshell the three things that make faith grow are Bible study, prayer, and good works. Let's see why!

Bible Study Helps Our Faith Grow

Romans 10:17 states that "faith cometh by hearing and hearing by the Word of God." Since faith comes from the Word of God, it is reasonable to assume that Bible

Study will also strengthen and enlarge our faith. The more we learn about Jesus in Bible Study, for example, the stronger our faith in him grows.

Prayer Helps Our Faith Grow

In mark 9:17-29, A man asked Jesus to heal his son whereupon Jesus said, "If you believe all things are possible." In tears, the father answered with a prayer: "Lord, I believe; help thou my unbelief!" Since Jesus <u>did</u> heal the boy, we know that the man's prayer was answered: his faith was made to grow by Jesus. And such a prayer <u>in Jesus'</u> name will work for us today because we know that Jesus does want our faith to grow.

Good Works Help Our Faith Grow

As pointed out already in James 2:20 we read that faith without works is dead. Since it is works that keeps faith alive; it is not unreasonable to assume that faith will also help a live faith grow. Then, too, by reading James 2:22, we see that works helped to perfect (make grow) Abraham's faith. But sometimes it takes a great deal of moral courage to do the good works for which we were created.

VIRTUE

As used in the Bible the word virtue has the meaning of both moral excellence and moral courage. It means living a life free from a <u>pattern</u> of sin and having enough courage to state Christian beliefs in spite of the threat of unpopularity and persecution. A good example of this type of virtue is seen in the words of the Apostle Peter after the Jewish authorities told him not to teach in the name of Jesus. Peter then said words to this effect, "it's right that we preach in Jesus' name, so we will listen to God and continue to preach." Will we have such courage to stand up against evil whether or not our position will make us unpopular? May God give us strength to do so.

KNOWLEDGE

Anything worth having is worth working for. This also applies to Bible knowledge. It takes effort, prayer, and research to dig from God's Word some of the most precious jewels of truth. But oh! What a joy when we behold the sparkling brilliance for which we prayed and worked so hard. And each Jewel uncovered helps us to grow stronger in our attempt to become a mature Christian.

TEMPERANCE (SELF CONTROL)

In olden days, the word temperance meant never to use alcohol. Today the meaning is broader than that. It means a proper and limited use of such earthly enjoyments as eating, sleeping, going to picture shows, and watching TV. It means keeping every sense under proper restraint and never letting the animal part overcome the use of good sense.

PATIENCE

This Christian grace has a <u>double meaning.</u> It means to bear all trials with an even mind—no flying off the handle and spitting fire. It also means to keep on keeping on in spite of disappointments, failures, and opposition. Patience is also called "steadfastness" or "perseverance" in some Bible versions and passages. How do we gain patience? James tells us how in James 1:3. We get patience by overcoming diverse temptations ("Diverse" has nothing to do with snorkeling; it means "several different kinds of temptation).

GODLINESS

Godliness means a deep reverence for God and a religious fear of displeasing him. It means not only worshipping God with every obedient outward act but also adoring and magnifying Him in our hearts. It means that just as a compass points to magnetic north so the spirit of the godly man always seem to be attracted to God.

BROTHERLY KINDNESS

Brotherly kindness means a strong feeling of attachment to the brotherhood, an earnest desire to provide the highest good for each of our brothers. Our deep affections lead us to love them as ourselves and gives us a desire to treat each of them by the "Golden Rule" (Matthew 7:12).

CHARITY

In I Corinthians 13:3, we see that we can give all our goods to feed the poor and still not have charity. Confusing? The word "charity" has changed in meaning since the King James Version of the <u>Bible</u> was written. At that time, the word charity simply meant "love." So we could give our goods to feed the poor without really loving them could we not? That's right we could.

Is love important? The answer is found in I Corinthians 13:1-3. Would you rate the person described below the same as God would rate him?

❖ Highly skilled in public speaking.
❖ Able to prophesy the future.
❖ Having a complete knowledge in all areas, including the Bible.
❖ Having faith strong enough to move mountains.

❖ Extremely generous in helping the poor.
❖ Willing to give his life for other people.

How would you rate this person, <u>if he did not have love?</u> How would God rate him? He would rate him just a noise (a sounding brass, a tinkling cymbal) nothing, and without profit for himself (a big fat zero on a scale from 1 to 10). Then how important is love? You answer the question!

But what does the word "love" really mean? Well, it depends on what type of love you are talking about. Four different Greek words with different meanings all have been translated as love in the Bible. Here they are:

❖ Eros – sexual, you hop in bed with me, Hollywood type of love.
❖ Phila – brotherly love.
❖ Storge – family type of love.
❖ Agape – the love that seeks the highest good for the individual.

Agape love is the type of love that God, Jesus and the Holy Spirit have for us. Sometimes, it is a "tough love." But always it seeks to encourage us to love and do good works, either by rewards or by punishment. This is the type of love that is described in I Corinthians 13:4-7; and since it is the crown jewel of the Christian graces, lets examine it in some detail. Here are the characteristics:

❖ Suffers long.
❖ Is kind.
❖ Does not envy.
❖ Does not brag or act arrogantly.
❖ Does not act unbecomingly.
❖ Does not seek its own.
❖ Is not provoked.
❖ Takes no account of evil.
❖ Does not rejoice in unrighteousness.
❖ Hopes all things.
❖ Believes all things.

❖ Endures all things.

Let's discuss each of these characteristics of love, telling what it means, describing a challenging condition, and giving examples of the wrong and right ways of handling the temptation.

Love Suffers Long

When offended, love does not explode into rash action or into a tirade of harsh words. Instead, love exhibits patience toward the offender, realizing that each of us is weak and prone to even weaker moments. Thus, love "keeps its cool" when provoked and speaks in a loving way, trying to rescue the offender from his sins.

The Challenge: You have discovered that a Christian has gossiped about you.

Wrong: Publicly you harshly rebuke the tale-bearing friend by telling him, "You are no longer my friend, you hypocritical, two-faced, foul-mouthed skunk. Please stay away from me. I can't afford to have a friend like you, you gossip." (Would this stop his gossip or cause him to repent?)

Right: When you and your friend are alone (Matthew 18:15), speaking the truth in a loving way, you could say, "John, you and I have been friends for a long time, and I value your friendship. John, it is hard for me to believe that you carried such a tale about me. You have hurt me deeply, John, but I forgive you. But more important, John, Jesus is displeased with your sins of tale bearing (Ephesians 4:31). And John, tale bearing is a public sin and you need to repent publicly. I'll be praying that you will." (Your main purpose here, brought about by your love, is to rescue your brother from Satan's grasp.)

Love Is Kind

With other people, love is as gentle as a nursing mother (I Thessalonians 2:7). Love is tenderhearted and forgiving (Ephesians 4:32). Even when it is offended, love shows a gentle and friendly spirit and shows good will to all men. Also, love is kind enough to overlook the flaws and defects of other people, realizing that each of us has a personal beam in his own eye (Matthew 7:3). Someone has said that "Love calls attention to the beautiful flowers beyond the broken gate" when visiting a friend.

The Challenge: You notice that a ten-year-old girl at church has come in ragged, dirty dress that is years out of fashion. [This is all she had.]

Wrong: Saying to the young girl: dear, this is God's house and we should put on our clean, best clothes. When you come here the next time, please dress appropriately. (See the tears flow? Will she ever come back to church again?)

Right: Give the young girl a hug and tell her you are glad she came. Tell her that you love to sew and that you have a pattern that will go well with such a pretty girl. Ask her if she will come to your house for a meal and for taking her sizes for a new dress.

Love Does Not Envy

Love rejoices at the good fortunes of others. Envy resents another person because of their good fortune or superior advantage. Because Joseph was favored by his father, his brothers envied him. Because Christ was popular with the common people, the Jewish leader delivered Him to Pilate and asked for Christ's crucifixion. Envy is rotten to the bone: Not only does envy lead to evil actions, but it affects both the happiness and the health of the person filled with envy (Proverbs 14:30). Where envy exists, there is disorder and every evil thing (James 3:16).

The Challenge: The judges of a contest that you entered have awarded Mary first prize.

Wrong: Tell Mary that you really deserved first prize and that the judges were wrong. Tell others that Mary probably bribed the judges.

Right: Rejoice with Mary for her victory (Romans 12:15). Congratulate her and in a good-natured tone tell her you will beat her next time.

Love Does Not Brag And Is Not Arrogant

Love does not feel or act superior to other people. Love does not make a showy display of its accomplishments. Love does not boast; boasting is the language of pride. Humility is the language of love. Love never does good for the purpose of receiving praise and for praising itself. Love bewares of practicing righteousness before men to be seen of them; otherwise, there is no reward from God (Matthew 6:1). Let him who boasts boast only in the Lord (I Corinthians 1:31).

The Challenge: You have just won first prize and are talking to the second-place winner.

Wrong: Looking superior, you say in a haughty tone: "I thought that I would win this time because my entry was a lot better than yours. And I'll probably beat you next time, too!"

Right: "You had a good entry and the contest was probably pretty close. I was lucky to win. Next time you may beat me."

Love Does Not Act Unbecomingly

Love displays good manners at all times and is careful not to offend other people by going against accepted customs in any particular situation. Love guards against using harsh and vulgar expressions which may hurt the feelings of the other people. Love tries to please other people <u>for their good and edification</u> (Romans 15:2).

<u>The Challenge:</u> A fellow Christian ask you a question about tonight's youth meeting while the Lord's Supper is being served.

<u>Wrong:</u> Quietly whisper to him: "We are to bring cokes and sandwiches. We will meet at Joe's house at 6:00 p.m."

<u>Right:</u> Quietly say to him: "Sh!"

Love Does Not Seek Its Own

Love is unselfish.   A Christian must be as concerned about the welfare of others as he is about his own welfare. A Christian does not insist on having his own way unless the other person's way would violate God's laws.   A Christian should love his neighbor as himself (Matthew 22:39), should look out for the interest of others (Philippians 2:4), and should see the good of his neighbor (I Corinthians 10:24).

<u>The Challenge:</u> While a Christian's neighbor is on an extended vacation, the Christian notices that the neighbors lawn is covered with several newspapers and his lawn is badly in need of mowing—an open invitation to burglars.

<u>Wrong:</u> The Christian should turn in his neighbor to the city so that the city will mow the lawn at the

neighbor's expense. The papers should be collected and placed in sacks for the city to haul away.

Right: Collect the papers <u>daily</u> and save them for the neighbor who might desire to read them. Mow the neighbor's lawn without telling him who did it.

Love Is Not Provoked
Love does not lose its temper. Is not irritable or bitter. Love does not harshly correct those who have wronged it. Love is quick to hear, slow to speak, and slow to anger (James 1:19,20). He who is slow to anger is better that the mighty and he who rules his spirit than he who captures a city (Proverbs 16:32).

The Challenge: After you have spent long, weary hours preparing a theme paper, a visiting friend ruins it by spilling a cup of coffee all over it.

Wrong: To impress your friend on the seriousness of his mistake you loudly exclaim, "You clumsy idiot, I spent 25 hours preparing that paper and your awkwardness ruined it because you didn't have enough sense to be careful." (Oh! Well! You didn't need that friend anyway! But what if you were trying to win him for Christ?)

Right: "Don't worry! I probably can copy it over in time to meet the deadline. I know how you feel—but don't feel ashamed: we all have done something like this and even worse at times."

Love Taketh No Account of Evil
Jesus said that we should forgive a brother who has sinned against us 7 X 70 (490) times. When he sins the 491st time we should then extract punishment for each of the 491 times. Right? No! Wrong! A Christian should

not need a spiritual CPA to make certain the books on sins are correctly balanced. But instead, Jesus meant that no matter how many times a brother sins against us we should forgive him. If we fail to forgive our brother from the heart each time, our own sins will not be forgiven and if we do completely forgive our brother from the heart each time, why do we need records of his sins against us or why need the service of a spiritual CPA (Matthew 18:32-35)?

The Challenge: A brother who had sinned against you, had repented and had been forgiven, has again committed the same sin against you, and now seeks forgiveness again.

Wrong: using a harsh tone to show the sinner the seriousness of his error, you tell them, "John, I thought you repented of this sin the last time. But since you have repeated the same sin, I wonder if you are playing the hypocrite? Make up your mind! Do you or do you not repent. If you do honestly repent, don't ever do it again.

Right: In a loving voice, filled with understanding, tell the sinner, "Of course I forgive you, John. I have sinned far more against Jesus than you have ever sinned against me. And if Jesus can forgive me of my many sins; I certainly can forgive you of your few. After all, I am not more important than Jesus."

Love Does Not Rejoice in Unrighteousness
A truly loving Christian does not rejoice when he hears that any man has fallen into sin, even if that man has wronged the Christian. A truly loving Christian does not "look down his nose" and feel superior to a sinner as the Pharisee did when praying near a publican (Luke 18:10-14). Jesus said the humble Publican was justified while the self-righteous Pharisee was not. And a truly loving

Christian would mourn for the vileness of the sinner, feel deep compassion for the sinner, and work and pray for the sinner's repentance.

The Challenge: A fellow Christian who has stolen your girlfriend has just been put in jail for drunk driving and striking a policeman.

Wrong: In speaking to the repentant brother who has been crying you say, "Your tears will do you no good if you go away from here and do it all over again. If you can't live a decent Christian life, don't disgrace the Lord by remaining a Christian; shape up, don't sin all over again. It makes you look like a hypocrite (After such a "message of love," what do you think the erring brother would do?).

Right: Giving the tearful repentant one a big hug, you say, "God bless you, John! Like you, we all sin at times. Pray for us and we will pray for you. God bless you."

Love Beareth All Things
The word "bear" comes from a Greek word actually meaning "to cover over." A Christian knows how to <u>keep silent</u> about evil which he sees, hears, or knows of anyone. He never reports evil unless duty demands it. His first report of evil is to <u>the affected sinner</u>, giving him a chance to confess and repent or to show that evil was not committed. A Christian never engages in gossip or tale bearing. Gossip and tale bearing stir up trouble and keep trouble going (Proverbs 26:20) and should not be tolerated among brethren.

The Challenge: A young widow is going from house to house spreading gossip, based mainly on unsubstantiated reports. You are trying to decide how to handle the situation.

Wrong: You tell the young widow, "Either stop your gossip or I will go to the home of each Christian and tell them about your sins; then I will make a public announcement in church about your tale bearing."

Right: Ask the young widow to meet you in a public place, supervised at a distance by other church members. Then explain to the widow that God hates tale-bearers, and that you have heard that she gossiped. Ask her if the report is true. If she confesses, ask her to repent publicly because of the public nature of her sins.

Love Believeth All Things

Love believes all the good it can about anyone, even though love is not blind to their faults. Love is not suspicious. Love believes that the actions of others are caused by the best motives and that other people do not intend injury or harm (I Corinthians 4:5).

The Challenge: Even though you and John have not been in any arguments, you do feel a tension between you and John whenever you are near each other. The last time this happened, John appeared to feel especially tense, turned on his heel, and rushed to speak to an elder.

Wrong: You rush to the elder, tell him about the tension between you and John and ask what John reported. The elder told you that John asked only about some material for working up a lesson for a class he was soon to be teaching (How red would your face be?).

Right: You believe that John was probably checking with the elder about some church business. At

the next opportunity, you should try to "break the ice" with John. After all, he is your brother in Christ.

Love Hopeth All Things
Love believes that the love, power, and grace of God can purify and brighten the corrupted image of God that lies buried within the heart of even the vilest sinner. Love believes that the gospel can lead any man or woman to repentance and good works.

The Challenge: While visiting a person, you meet a man who is a habitual criminal, who seems to be constantly mad at the world, and whose every word seems to be cursing, including taking the Lord's name in vain.

Wrong: He's too far gone; beyond redemption. There is no use wasting our time on him.

Right: The gospel can work on even the hardest heart if we allow God's power to work through us. (By the way, this is an actual case, and the hardened criminal did become a Christian.)

Love Endureth All Things
Even though the wrongs done seem endless, true love continues to work for the good of the other person. Imbedded in this love is the belief that eventually the wrong doer will change (Just ask any parent who has raised a child to maturity). We should forgive a person an endless number of times (Matthew 18:21, 22). Remember how patient that God is with us (II Peter 3:9).

The Challenge: A friend of yours is in the habit of stealing money from your billfold. He does confess his sin each time he steals money and requests your forgiveness. He now stands before you, confessing his sin again.

<u>Wrong:</u> You say to your friend, "Theophrastus, you have done this once too often. I don't believe that I can ever trust you again. Our friendship is at an end. Please, you go your way and I'll go mine."

<u>Right:</u> You say to your friend, "Yes, my friend I forgive you, but this sin seems to bother you a great deal. Let's you and I pray that you will have the strength to resist the temptation in the future. With Jesus' help, you will have the strength to overcome this besetting sin.

So much for our discussion of the Christian graces. How much have you learned? Test your knowledge by working the following exercises.

<u>Section II: Let's See What You've Learned</u>

1. How does the expression "Nature abhors a vacuum" apply in a spiritual sense? _____

_____

_____

2. As we grow in the Christian graces, we become more and more like _____

_____

(II Peter 1:4)

3. What will growing and abounding in the Christian graces help to prevent? _____

_____

_____

4. The two types of faith are _____and

_____

(Ephesians 4:4)

5. Faith is the _____

   hoped for and the _____

   not seen (Hebrews 11:1)

6. What is meant by the expression "a saving faith" (John
   3:16, Hebrew 5:9) _____

   _____

   _____

   _____

7. What two things related to faith must we believe in
   order to please God? _____

   _____

   (Hebrews 11:6)

8. What does it mean to "diligently seek God?"

   _____

   _____

   _____

9. What is the only thing that can separate us from God?

   _____

   _____

   (Isaiah 59:2)

10. What three things will help faith grow?

   _____,

_____ and

_____

11. What is meant by the Christian grace of virtue?
_____ and

_____

_____

12. What is meant by temperance (self control)?
_____

_____

_____

13. The two meanings of the word patience are
_____ and

_____

_____

14. The word "godliness" has the outward meaning of
_____ _____ and the
inward meaning of _____

15. What is the relationship between brotherly kindness and
the "golden rule"? _____
_____

_____

_____

16. In today's language, the word substituted for "charity" (as used in the King James version of the Bible) is

_____

17. How do you know that love is important

_____

_____

(I Corinthians 13:1-3)

18. What types of love are sinless for an unmarried Christian _____ , _____ and

_____

19. What type of love does Jesus have for us?

_____

20. How should a Christian react to a brother who has sinned against him? _____

_____

_____

21. What is kindness? _____

_____

22. What harm is done by envy? _____

_____

23. What reaction follows a braggart? Man's reaction _____ God's reaction

_____

24. Why should a Christian always exhibit good manners?

_____

_____

_____

25. When should a Christian stubbornly insist on having things "his" way? _____

_____

_____

26. What harm can result from losing your temper?

_____

_____

_____

27. How many times should your forgive your brother in Christ? _____

_____

28. Should we feel superior to a Christian who has fallen into sin? Explain _____

_____

_____

29. When a sinner publicly repents, how should we feel?

_____

_____

(Luke 15:7)

30. How should you react if you know a "juicy" secret about the failings of another Christian?

_____

_____

_____

31. What attitude should a Christian have concerning the reason for another Christian's action? _____

_____

32. What limits the effects of the gospel in converting the vilest of sinners? _____

_____

_____

33. Why do parents endure the seemingly endless wrong they see in raising children? _____

_____

_____ Is there a lesson in this for us Christians? If so, what lesson? _____

_____

Section III: Now Let's Get Personal

1. On the line after each of the Christian graces, indicate how you will make any necessary changes in that grace.

    a. Faith _____

    _____

b. Virtue _____

_____

c. Knowledge _____

_____

d. Self control _____

_____

e. Patience _____

_____

f. Godliness _____

_____

g. Brotherly Kindness _____

_____

h. Love _____

_____

2. Measure yourself answering the following questions:
    a. With prayerful thought, answer each of the following questions by placing a check mark in the appropriate column to indicate yes, usually, seldom, or no.
    b. Ask another member of your family or a friend to answer the same questions and discuss any differences in answers (no fisticuffs, please!)
    c. Pick out your weakest areas (the NO answers) and work and pray to overcome them – one at a time.

    d. Then work on the questions answered "seldom" and finally on the questions answered "usually".

COMMENT

For most of us, this will lay out a year-long program of growth in love and will demand constant attention, hard work, and many hours of prayer. But the GOAL – to be like Christ and live someday with Him in heaven – is certainly worth the price, isn't it?

QUESTIONS YES USUALLY   SELDOM   NO

1. Do you display endless patience toward the weakness, ridicule, criticism, and slights of other people

    ___   ___   ___   ___

2. Are you patient toward your own weaknesses?

    ___   ___   ___   ___

3. Do you accept the delays of God in accomplishing his purposes–without murmuring or complaining

    ___   ___   ___   ___

QUESTIONS YES USUALLY SELDOM NO

4. Are you careful not to hurt the feelings of others?

_____   _____   _____   _____

5. Do you display good manners at all times?

_____   _____   _____   _____

6. Do you rejoice when another receives more
honor than you?

_____   _____   _____   _____

7. Do you fight the desire to seek the applause of men?

_____   _____   _____   _____

8. Do you fee that you do not truly deserve all your
blessings?

_____   _____   _____   _____

9. Do you avoid bluntness and loud-mouthed clowning?

_____   _____   _____   _____

10. Are you truly concerned for the welfare, comfort and
salvation of other people?

_____   _____   _____   _____

11. Are you slow to be offended, to show displeasure and
to develop grudges?

_____   _____   _____   _____

12. Do you always judge the motives of other people
favorably?

_____   _____   _____   _____

QUESTIONS   YES   USUALLY   SELDOM   NO

13.   Are you saddened when a person who has mistreated you meets with embarrassment, discomfort, or misfortune?

____   ____   ____   ____

14. Does your heart swell with joy when a brother repents or a sinner is baptized?

____   ____   ____   ____

15.   Do you refuse to betray secrets or talk about the sins and faults of others?

____   ____   ____   ____

16.   Do you try to overlook the imperfections of others and to avoid pointing them out?

____   ____   ____   ____

17. When a vicious sinner repents, do you always believe they really mean it?

____   ____   ____   ____

18.   When a person apologizes to you, do you always believe they really mean it, even if they apologized several times before for the same error ?

____   ____   ____   ____

19. Do you believe that even the most hard-hearted sinner can be reached by the Gospel - if YOU take it to him ?

____   ____   ____   ____

George J. Cunningham, Sr.

YOU SAY YOU LOVE ME
You say you love me with all of your heart
In accents soft and sweet,
My beauty and majesty you adore,
And I am your heart complete.

Oh, what do your actions say?
Are you living for me each day?
Is the life that you live a love song?
Oh, what do your actions say?"

You say you love me and I am your joy
When we are alone in prayer,
But when strangers to me are passing your way,
Do you tell them of my beauty fair?

You say you love me and I am your Lord,
Your master to obey.
If joys I forbid you relish each day—
Oh! What do your actions say?

You say you love me and my tender heart,
The forgiveness I display.
If you harden your heart and foul it with hate
Oh! What do your actions say?

You say you love me and my sacrifice,
You sing of it night and day.
If you won't give me your time and your wealth,
Oh! What do your actions say?

Oh! What do your actions say?
Are you living for me each day?
Is the life that you live a love song?
Oh! What do your actions say?
                    —George J. Cunningham—

BOOKS OF THE BIBLE
LISTED ALPHABETICALLY

PAGE NO. (Page Number); N in this column (New Testament)

NAME	PAGE	NAME	PAGE
ACTS	N _____	HAGGIA	_____
AMOS	_____	HEBREWS	N _____
I CHRONICLE	_____	HOSEA	_____
II CHRONICLES	_____	ISAIAH	_____
COLOSSIANS	N _____	JAMES	N _____
I CORINTHIANS	N _____	JEREMIAH	_____
II CORINTHIANS	N _____	JOB	_____
DANIEL	_____	JOEL	_____
DEUTERONOMY	_____	JOHN	N _____
ECCLESIANSTES	_____	I JOHN	N _____
EPHESIANS	N _____	II JOHN	N _____
ESTHER	_____	III JOHN	N _____
EXODUS	_____	JONAH	_____
EZEKIEL	_____	JOSHUA	_____
EZRA	_____	JUDGES	_____
GALATIANS	N _____	JUDE	N _____
GENESIS	_____	I KINGS	_____
HABAKKUK	_____	II KINGS	_____
LAMENTATION	_____	PROVERBS	_____
LEVITICUS	_____	PSALMS	_____
LUKE	N _____	REVELATIONS	N _____
MALACHI	_____	ROMANS	N _____
MARK	N _____	RUTH	_____
MATTHEW	N _____	I SAMUEL	_____
MICAH	_____	II SAMUEL	_____
NAHUM	_____	SONG OF SOLOMON	_____
NEHEMIAH	_____	I THESSALONIANS	N _____

BOOKS OF THE BIBLE
LISTED ALPHABETICALLY

PAGE NO. (Page Number); N in this column (New Testament)

KISS THE WHIP

1. I Kiss the whip that scourges me, my sonship to assure.
    For chast'ning which thou givest me to keep my spirit pure.
    I praise thee for thy care divine: a conscience pricking me.
    In tearful joy, I lift mine eyes to pour my thanks to thee.
2. I kiss the whip that scourges me, my growing to promote.
    Temptations which I overcome by strength which thou devote.
    I praise thee for they care divine, steadfast giving me.
    In tearful joy, I lift mine eyes to pour my thanks to thee.
3. I kiss the whip that scourges me, to give to me thy peace.
    For worldly mock, abuse, and pain—my patience to increase.
    I praise thee for they care divine, exciting love in me
    In tearful joy; I lift mine eyes to pour my thanks to thee.
4. I kiss the whip that scourges me, that cuts me to the heart
    Beloved brothers doubting me that mine eyelids smart
    I praise thee for thy care divine, a balm of peace to me
    In tearful joy, I lift mine eyes to pour my thanks to thee.
5. I kiss the whip that scourges me, when death doth from me part
6. The dear ones oh so near and sweet to mine own aching heart
    I praise thee for thy care divine: I know 'tis best for me
    In tearful joy, I lift mine eyes to pour my thanks to thee.
    (continued)

Chorus
> Oh, Lord, my God, I love thee so, come losses or come gain
> Bless me like Job, to love thee still in sorrow or in pain
> Thy will be done, for thou alone life's pattern understand
> And give each moment what is best to mold me to thy plan.

—George J. Cunningham—

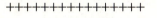

Keep Me Wise

I am weak, oh my Lord and allured by the world.
In temptation, I stumble about.
Give me strength to endure and to keep my life pure.
Give me strength, oh my Lord, give me strength.
Chorus:

Keep me wise, to realize, that a vict'ry, when won, is not mine.
'Tis a gift from above coming down with thy love.
Keep me thankful and wise, oh my Lord

I am stained by my thought, dark and loathsome my heart;
And for cleansing I plea, oh I plea.
Give me pardon, I pray, purify thou my way.
Give me pureness of heart, oh my Lord.

I am fouled by my hate, malice will not abate;
Mercy seems not to live in my heart.
And condemned do I stand by my cold vengeful heart.
Grant me grace to forgive, oh my Lord.
(continued)

I am wayward my Lord, wand' ring from thee it seems
And I slip far away from the fold.
Draw me back to thy side – Heart of iron in that I have –
Love, the magnet, is thine, oh my Lord.

I am blessed, oh my Lord, with a bounty so sweet;
And my heart often says, "It is mine."
Keep me mindful each day that the good things I have
Are not to mine but a free gift from thee.

Chorus

Keep the wise, to realize, that a vict'ry when won, is not
mine.
'Tis a gift from above coming down with thy love.
Keep me thankful and wise, oh my Lord.

--George J. Cunningham--